Stories and Stor

Angela M. Keyes

Alpha Editions

This edition published in 2024

ISBN : 9789362518026

Design and Setting By
Alpha Editions
www.alphaedis.com
Email - info@alphaedis.com

As per information held with us this book is in Public Domain.
This book is a reproduction of an important historical work. Alpha Editions uses the best technology to reproduce historical work in the same manner it was first published to preserve its original nature. Any marks or number seen are left intentionally to preserve its true form.

PREFACE

All the stories in this book have been tested with children. Favorites easily available in other collections have been omitted.

The seventy-five or more very short stories, intended to help young children to express their observations, experiences, and fancies, have been included at the request of many teachers.

The writer hopes that by providing the busy teacher with "tellable" stories, she may help to win for story-telling the dignity of established scholastic place.

STORY-TELLING

With high esteem and full of respect I greet a genuine story-teller; with intense gratitude I grasp him by the hand.

—Froebel

The school is joining hands with the children for fuller recognition of the story and story-telling.

Note, by the way, that it is with the children. In an elder day grown-ups, too, yielded themselves to the witchery of the story. But printing and the book banished the wandering story-teller; with a little progress in science came recoil from the superstitions and absurdities of the folk tale; the increasing complexity of life bred in the superficial thinker contempt for the unperplexed nursery fable; the intellectual pedant found it distressingly naïve; pressure of affairs robbed the busy man of any leisure for it. So, among peoples advancing in civilization, the grown-ups gradually left the story more and more to the children. And the children, wise youngsters that they are, have never allowed themselves to outgrow it.

Is it not delightful to note that learning is bringing the adult back to the story? The trend of thought to-day, urging him to look to the natural beginnings of things, is taking him back to the story. The historian searches it for early glimpses of fact; the philosopher sees lasting wisdom in it; the literary seer marvels at the truth and beauty of fairy-tale symbols of life; the busy man of affairs accompanies his children to juvenile drama and nonsense opera. The art of story-telling itself is again finding an audience among men and women, as well as children. Best of all, the school, directing its effort toward the natural development of the young child, is pressing the educational properties of the story.

Reiteration of these properties now is timely. Psychology is throwing clearer light on the education of the feelings and the taste; the story should be helpful here. The thoughtful in the community are urging more attention to the spiritualizing and humanizing subjects in the courses of study; the story belongs in this class. Other favorable present conditions will appear as the merits of the story are briefly set forth.

The story and story-telling will

(1) *Give pleasure.*

(2) *Stir and direct the imagination.*

(3) *Arouse and direct the feelings.*

(4) *Cultivate the taste.*

(5) *Help to shape thought and language mode.*

(6) *Stimulate and direct potential literary creativity.*

(7) *Serve as foreword for book-study of literature.*

(8) *Give knowledge of life.*

(1) *The story will give pleasure.* Educational thought is growing more and more cordial toward this value. Undisturbed by any charge of "soft pedagogy," it finds wholesome pleasure, not merely relaxing, but constructive, building toward physical health, mental brightness, and moral virtue. Here is the story's opportunity. Every one admits it is pleasure-giving. The stern-minded among us must realize that this is its deepest educational value. It is from the good pleasure the child gets from the story that will ripen good taste, good will, good effort, and all the other goods some teachers and parents regard as more substantial merit. Besides, joy appears to be here to stay. To attempt to take it out of the plan of things is, to say the least, short-sighted. American civilization is looking hopefully to the school for better national standards of pleasure. The school is under obligation to educate the children to enjoyment of wholesome pleasure.

(2) *The story will stir and direct the imagination.* We do not yet grant in practice the importance of the imagination. We do not purposefully exercise it, as we do, for example, the reason. We say glibly that imagination is at the root of the successful man's arrival at material profit, of the explorer's discovery and the practical scientist's invention, of the poet's song and the philanthropist's vision of a state of society in which the kingdom of heaven will be nearer at hand; but we give little or no training to the imagination. Here again is the story's opportunity. Through the story the interpretative story-teller may give the imagination consistent exercise.

(3) *The story will arouse and direct the pupil's feelings.* The school to-day is emphasizing the necessity of educating the heart, the climactic third of the three great H's,—the Head, the Hand, and the Heart. And psychologists are telling us that to educate a child to be kind, unselfish, filial, reverent, gentle, courageous, good-tempered, to educate him to admire goodness, justice, valor, to be sensible of beauty, to aspire and make effort toward excellence, is as practicable as to train him to do or to make something. It

calls for more delicate but not different treatment; working not by dictation, but by magnetic suggestion. The story-teller may render a great service to the individual and to the community by helping to form right feeling-habit.

(4) *The well-chosen story will cultivate the taste.* Psychology is urging early direction also of the æsthetic sense. The story-teller, through her own joyous response to beauty, has it in her power to awaken and direct the children's appreciation of beauty. It is she, too, who must help to lay the foundation for that better taste in novel or play that America eagerly desires, and that publisher and playwright say they stand ready to satisfy as soon as the public arrives at it.

(5) *The story will help to form the child's thought and language habit.* As this is the value most often acknowledged in classroom practice—though not always by the best methods—it is not necessary to do more at this point than restate it. Mastery in thought and language is far-reaching usefulness, affecting individual growth and social harmony. The story, because of its easy, more or less artless composition and graphic diction, lends itself to starting right thought and language mode.

(6) *Story-telling may help to stimulate and direct potential literary creativity.* In spite of its breadth of view the school appears insensible to the rights of children born creative. The array of geniuses recently marshaled by a Chicago professor, that teachers pronounced hopeless dunces and in some cases drove from their classes, should set the school thinking. It is reaching out helpful hands to the little unfortunate ones, the blind and the deaf and the sick; but it continues to dismiss the divinely commissioned little sister or brother, with the platitude that his genius will survive if it be sufficiently sturdy. This is a specious half-truth unworthy of repetition. It is, besides, discrimination against the individual. The school is not meeting its obligation to *all* the children of the community. It will not do to lay the blame to the community's "commercialized" standards. In spite of apparent emphasis on the useful arts, the community would not lose from the varied web of its civilization the bright thread of painting and music and story. Maturing thought is convincing it that the fine arts are finely utilitarian. Here, again, is the story's opportunity. The simple materials and childlike fancy in it may stimulate gradually and naturally play of the creative imagination.

(7) *Story-telling should be at least foreword for book-study of literature.* The thoughtful teacher of literature to-day finds in the classic story all the elements of her material, and sees in the child listening to it the most promising student of literature. At the freely sympathetic period the child becomes familiar with the inner life of language as used to represent

fundamental motive, character, and action. This is precisely the kind of knowledge that he should bring as basis for study of more advanced literature. The printed page will be informed with lively meaning, to which his imagination, feeling, and æsthetic sense can respond. It is largely the school's neglect of oral foundation in literature, which, by the way, should not be confined to the lowest grades, that is at the root of feeble appreciation in book-study of literature.

(8) The story holds in it a greater value, as much greater as life is than literature; *it will give knowledge of life*. The writer might have said experience of life, because of the child's strong tendency to be and to do what attracts him. Students of literature, to-day, are urging that it is not a mere "polishing" study, but the substantially useful subject from which we may get clear and inspiring knowledge of life. They would have literature recognized as the reflection of life, idealized, it may be, but therefore stronger reflection. As life is the occupation that all of us, no matter what our special vocation may be, must engage in together, a study that throws light on it is indispensable. Here is a great opportunity for the story. Every genuine story, sense or nonsense, is a glimpse of life, which will early give guiding knowledge and experience.

The story-teller cannot, by the way, afford to ignore the evil in life. You may have read the story of Kipling's "kid"; how the parents in fond but foolish love for their only son shut away from him all knowledge that evil has come into the world, and how the son, grown to manhood, enters army life, where he meets his first temptation and falls. The moral of the tale is obvious. Though it is wise to keep in the wake of their experience with evil, the story should help to provide the children with knowledge and modes of conduct for the situations of real life. The cunning story-teller, presenting this or that bit of life, from which he has not made the mistake of taking out the evil already within the child's experience or presently to be met, touches the child into recoil from evil and into admiration and imitation of the triumphant way of virtue.

The story should, however, oftener engage children's attention with good, rather than evil, as the central, active force in life. And the story told to the growing boy or girl, and to the youth, should prompt him to fine and finer endeavor. It is a fatal error to assume that teachers and parents cannot help to raise the community's standards, that the best the rising generation may carry out from home and school is negative prudence, readiness to accept questionable social practices and ideals, that they themselves may achieve worldly success. If each generation does not leave the world a little better for its part in it, it has lived in vain, and its "guides, philosophers, and friends," the parents and teachers of it, have denied their office. The story helping toward this kind of constructivity should lead. It is to the habit formed in its children that society must look for higher standards of living.

The story will widen the child's outlook on life. On the wings of the word the listener may fly away to the uttermost bounds of the earth. In the story world he, if poor, may be rich; if sad, merry; if inarticulate, he may find expression.

Though it is not exhaustive, this is an imposing array of reasons for admitting the story to unquestioned educational dignity. If the school feel the need of broad, scholarly precedent, it may find it in the work or in the recorded opinions of such seers as the Lambs, Longfellow, Carroll, Hawthorne, Scott, Stevenson, Browning, Ruskin, Froebel, Emerson. As yet story-telling is largely left optional with the teacher. Should it not be made a delightful school requirement? It addresses itself, it is true, mainly to the æsthetic taste and the feelings, it does not guarantee consequent action. But give it place early enough, and, if it must bring it, the other good effect will be added unto it.

The best reason for admitting the story to scholastic dignity still remains the best, its lasting charm for the children.

Kinds of Stories to Tell

We appear to be coming to the agreement that we should tell the children many of the old, old stories and some of the new, many stories from the world of the imagination, some from the real world; stories that will aid them in interpreting their world, themselves, other children, some grown-ups, nature; stories that will direct aright the imagination, the sympathies, and the taste; playful stories and more serious, sensible and nonsensical; short stories and longer; stories to be told over and over again, stories to be told in passing. To meet the child's and later the girl's and boy's changing tastes and interests, and the needs of their developing imagination and sympathies, our choice should embrace, besides a great many others that as yet have eluded classification, fairy tales, fables, myths, legends, romances, tales of adventure, stories of animal life, child life, growing boy and girl life, stories of great men and women.

Some teachers find it hard to see any educational value in play-stories like "The Three Bears," nonsense stories like "Chicken-Licken," and drolls, or farce "funny" stories like "Lazy Jack." They do not get the child's point of view. They are disturbed by the apparently idle pleasure or extravagance of them. "Chicken-Licken" appears to be nothing but driveling nonsense. The writer has no desire to attempt to turn it into sense nor to press unduly the claim of this particular type of story. But why not let it in as a nonsense tale, an opportunity for giving the mind a frolic? This is advanced by some students of the tale as its possible origin. It may be thought of as a reflection in literature of the naïveté of childhood; it catches capitally its guilelessness in motive, social intercourse, and deed. Its form also is childlike. The child ekes out invention in the manner of the tale, by the open artifice of cumulation and repetition. Or the story may be dignified into literary introduction to that type of classic which records the very common human situation, "much ado about nothing."

The same teachers are disturbed also by the ethical code of many of the folk tales; they find it crude and fleshly. It deals in large and sense-delighting rewards. But may it not be possible that the child must be allowed time to grow to a more discriminating standard of conduct and a finer kind of satisfaction?

It is to be hoped, however, that even then the child will retain his capacity for laughing at merry play and hearty comedy. Laughter is good for the world. It is a tonic to the emotions, and regeneration to the spirit, spurring it to fresh and better effort; it is a sign, too, of broadening imagination and sympathy. The man that has no laughter in him is like Shakespeare's man that has no music in him, "fit for treasons, stratagems, and spoils. Let no such man be trusted." Most stories will give the children a more reserved pleasure, happy mental and æsthetic satisfaction; some a fine gladness and exaltation. But let us not be too narrow to admit the wholesomely "funny" story.

The over-strained, anæmic, goody-good story is likely to breed up a generation of canting hypocrites. The little child is much occupied, it is true, with the task of being good, and he is a great admirer of the good people in the stories. There is room in children's literature for the rather obviously moral tale, if it be not too often presented and if it be really charming. From this point of view, Constance D'Arcy Mackay's book of plays called "The House of the Heart and Other Tales" is a suggestive contribution to children's drama.

For the younger children the story with plenty of action, often with animals as characters, and with happy ending has proved best. The story with less joyous "inevitable ending" is, however, not to be excluded; life is not to be distorted. Besides, not all sad-ending stories are negative in effect, leaving the child knowing only "what not to do" rather than "what to do." A story like Hans Andersen's "Daisy," for example, induces constructive inference and effect.

THE PRINCIPLES OF THE ART OF TELLING STORIES

Story-telling is one of the most spontaneous of the social arts. Yet it is an art, governed by at least partially discerned principles. Analysis of them will be helpful to the story-teller, but only in so far as he grasps the fundamental principle that story telling among the speech arts, like wood-carving among the manual arts, indeed, even to a greater degree, must be kept what it is by nature, apparently without art, naïve and unelaborate.

GETTING THE STORY

The story-teller must wholly take into himself the life of which he speaks, must let it live and operate in himself freely.

—FROEBEL.

The story-teller must himself possess the story before attempting to give it to another. This sounds obvious, but it is not granted in practice. Much poor schoolroom story-telling is evidently "unprepared." People born with a natural turn for story-telling, and those who in their childhood heard real story-telling, need to make less preparation than others; but all story-tellers need to make preparation. Much of the story-telling masquerading as such is quackery, showing neither genius nor study. Even in the very early days when formal instruction in story-telling was unknown, the wandering story-teller watched constantly to make his performance tell, modifying his method in the light of its effect upon his hearers. Later on, in the Middle Ages, the court story-teller was professionally trained (and also handsomely remunerated and given the place of honor at the banquet). Intellectual study of the story will not, by the way, destroy spontaneity. It may dash it temporarily. Coleridge tells us that his professor in poetics did not hesitate to subject to the scrutiny of the microscope the most delicate flowers and fruits of fancy. (English in the schools has suffered from the results, in its teachers, of the "literary affectation," which condemns attempt at definite English scholarship.) Let us give all outlet possible to natural ability, and to the inspiration of time and audience; but let us not neglect the forethought of preparation. Shakespeare did not, Sir Henry Irving did not, Duse does not. Some teachers fall back on reading the story; this has its own place, but it cannot take the place of telling. The belief that story-telling should be studied is gaining ground in a most convincing quarter, the home. The office of motherhood is deeply associated with things done instinctively right; but the mother herself at mothers' clubs and elsewhere is seeking instruction in this chief mother art.

To get the story, relax your imagination and sympathy and let them go out to it. Sit down with it and read and re-read it, or listen to it, and brood upon it until you absorb its life, until you think and feel and move in its being. Conjure up its scene and people and happening.

Some may find imagining difficult. Perhaps it was neglected in their training. Let them not be discouraged; each succeeding attempt to realize scene and person and action will make the task easier.

You may, by the way, study the story in either of two places: a lovely natural spot, where under the lure of century-wisdomed tree, or amid sweet smells, or flash of birds, or beckonings of shadows, you may catch the glamour of the old-world setting in the stories; or in a city street swarming with children, old-faced before their time. The environment in the second studio, far from destroying your effort to grasp the wonder-world of the story, will make special appeal to you. Here you will feel divine compulsion to make child life more abundant: to bring from story land bright hosts of gay fairies and gentle children and brave knights and real as well as fiction heroes as saving company for the little worldlings, to make them chuckle with a child's hearty glee at trick of goblin or sprite, or quake with delicious tremor at the tread of the terrible giant. You will find that the "toughest," most crabbed city urchin will succumb to the witchery of the fairy folk, to the charm of beauty and the fair play of kindness and honesty.

The child's world reflected in the story is the right of the child in the city tenement district, and society's hope for him. It is, by the way, no less the right of the rich child and no less society's hope for him.

After you have let the story take possession of you, take possession of it. To take possession of the story,

(1) *Seek its spirit and intention.*

(2) *Grasp its elements; its setting, its action, its characters.*

(3) *Master its workmanship, or its composition and style.*

Its spirit and intention. Students of folklore hesitate to impose on the folk tales ethical or æsthetical motive; but they would not object to our seeing in them, in addition to certain primitive ideas, this or that playful fancy or more serious reflection of life; in "The Elves and the Shoemaker," for example, hearty testimony to the worth of honest effort, the record raised to some degree of æsthetic merit by the charm of elfin appreciation; in "Star Dollars," crude sketch of childlike goodness and faith, the picture touched into beauty by the benediction of heaven; lovely symbol of gentle living, like "Diamonds and Toads"; sweet blossom of immortal beauty and goodness blighted by the withering poison of envy, yet triumphantly blooming, like "Snow White;" simple appreciation of kindness of heart, like the "Hut in the Wood;" idyl of the beauty and integrity of goodness, like "Beauty and the Beast;" in "The Straw, the Coal, and the Bean," naïve history of a merry-tragic situation; in "The Wolf and the Seven Kids," the happy triumph of mother wit sharpened by love. For the children they, as well as the more modern tales, must be kept direct, simple stories. But the student need not miss a broader significance. He can hardly fail to appreciate the analogies to human conduct so often implied in Hans Andersen's tales, done, as in Dante's great tale, with conscious intent. He must not, however, ask the children to probe for hidden meanings, and he must not strain at suggesting them in his interpretation. The story is not to be turned into an abstraction; its concreteness is the secret of its power to please and to move.

After you have thus characterized the story to yourself, grasp its elements: its setting, or time and place; its action; its persons, or characters. And cultivate sensibility to their appropriateness.

The setting. The lovely fairy romances, old and new, like "The Frog Prince," "Cinderella," Andersen's "Princess on the Pea," occurred in the all-possible "once upon a time," or in that delectable bygone when "wishing was having," or in such right good kingly times as Arthur's or Charlemagne's. Sometimes the place was an enchanted castle shut away behind a hedge of thorns and trees, in the very heart of a forest, a hedge that sprang up in a quarter of an hour, with thorns long enough to impale unworthy suitors; sometimes it was the highroad out to the world, upon which many a stout hero set foot to seek fortune. The merry gallant history of "Tom Thumb," fairy fledgeling, wizard-fostered, king's jester and doughty knightling, is referred to the magical days of Merlin and the chivalrous court of Arthur. We find him, too, versatile little imp, in his mother's practical pudding bowl, in the red cow's mouth, in a giant's stomach, inside a fish; and each place is capital setting for him. Who says that giants are figments of the imagination? The people of Cornwall record that it was in their land that Jack killed the giant, and they point out a castle built on a rock standing in the sea as the stronghold of the monster. (Let the folklorists find in this primitive belief, if they will; let us find, also, artistic fitness.) What a delightful plausibility the tale takes on from this minutely recorded geographical setting, as delightful in its way as the vague long ago and dim place of other tales! Here, in the apparently artless tale, is the artistic device by which Defoe hoodwinked the England of his day into believing that Robinson Crusoe was fact and not truer fiction.

Note the appropriateness in change of scene; Andersen's "Ugly Duckling," among the modern tales, affords a good study. The artistic principle is applied more naïvely in the old story of "The Hut in the Wood" at the transformation of the hut into a castle to be fit setting for the sovereign power and beauty of kindness; also in "Mother Holle," at the emergence of the child from the dark well and darker despair into the lovely meadow where the sun was shining, and thousands of flowers were blooming, and wonderful little ovens and red apple-trees called out to her, and golden shower fell on her and glorified her. In "Dummling," at the stage when enchantment is brought in, the scene changes completely to a stone castle in whose courtyard are stalls containing stone horses.

Note the narrative use made of setting. The appearance of the sea, in "The Fisherman and his Wife," as the fisherman carries each succeeding wish of his wife to the flounder, does as much to tell the story as the action itself.

Setting, then, is part of the whole. It is not to be overdone, nor is any part in the simple story, but its appropriateness is worth appreciation.

The action. The action is of course the chief part of the story. The motive of the action is easy to find. But again note that it is faithful to life and that it paves the way for appreciation of the motives of greater literature. In the simple tales, as in the novel and the drama, the action arises from love, hate, envy, spirit of adventure, friendship, malice, spirit of fun and play. Grasp the details of the action. In some versions of "The Frog Prince" the falling of the princess's golden ball into the well is made the occasion for the appearance of the magical frog, which, for the aid he offers, imposes the condition of companionship and love. The princess pretends agreement. Her repugnance to the frog becomes the complicating force. And (in some tales) her father's insistence that she keep her promise to the frog makes all come out happily; the frog stands revealed a prince in disguise, and marries the princess. In "Dummling" the despised stupid third and youngest brother sets out to seek his elders; then come the three acts of unkindness he prevents; then the failure of the elders at the task set forth in the enchanted castle, and Dummling's success, due to the aid of the creatures to whom he had shown kindness, followed by his triumphant marriage to the youngest and dearest of the princesses. In "The Cat and the Mouse in Partnership," the story opens with the doubtful compact entered into by the mouse on the cat's representation of friendship, and her agreement to his proposal that they lay by a pot of fat for the winter. The cat has the hardihood to propose the church as the safest hiding place for the pot of fat, hypocritically saying that no one would dare steal anything from a church. Then comes the cat's first "gulling" of the frank little mouse with his story of having been asked to be godfather to his cousin's remarkable child. "Beauty and the Beast" is another good character study, and from an important point of view for the little child's story a better one, as this time virtue is unmistakably triumphant.

The student will gradually develop sensibility to the typical materials of folk story: human difficulty overcome by supernatural aid; the task of guessing a name, or the forfeit of a child, as a condition for aid, as in

"Rumpelstiltskin;" trial and triumph of the despised ugly third sister or stupid third brother; doughty deeds that overcome bulk of body with nimbleness of wit, as in "Jack the Giant Killer;" greed of wishing whose indulgence precipitates loss of all, as in "The Fisherman and his Wife;" reward of kindness to animals, as in "The Hut in the Wood."

The characters. Characterize the people in the story. In their varied company is the story-teller's opportunity to acquaint the child with the chief kinds of persons to be found in literature and life; the child himself, cherishing mother, doting grandmother, virile father sending his sons out to find their place in the world, loving brother and sister, gentle people, hateful people, ill-tempered people, cruel people, jealous people, kind people, wily people, frank people, brave people, cowards, old people, children, sad people, merry people. Besides these, animals, pigs and bears, cows and hens and goats, inhabit the child's world side by side with man, helping the story to make its way to the child's affections. Then there is the host of witching fairy folk: fairies, giants, elves, pixies, witches, goblins. Music as well as language has attempted to suggest them, and with surprising agreement in artistic convention. Language makes fairies light, airy, tripping; goblins, grotesque; so does music. Language makes the giant huge, clumsy, big-handed and big-footed, but stupid; Wagner gives ponderous musical motif to the dragon, the "laidly worm," the giant of his music dramas, and also makes him conquerable.

The workmanship, composition, and style. Much story-telling is spoiled by disregard of the *composition* of the narrative. By composition here is meant what is meant in painting or sculpture, the arranging, or grouping, of the materials, to build out the whole.

The method of grouping in the folk story is apparent. At the beginning of the story are the time and place, some of the principal characters, and the motive of the action. Next follows the action, easily separable into rise, course, resolution. In many of the stories, for example, in "The Frog Prince," there is after the action an explanation of enchantment; and an assurance that all went well ever after or quaint formula like that parodied in "They stepped on a tin, and the tin bended, so my story's ended," whose purpose, similar to that of Shakespeare's rhyming couplet in his earlier dramas, is to give conclusive ending to the tale. Like "Mrs. Wiggs of the Cabbage Patch," who stayed on at the theater after the curtain had gone down on the last scene, the children, though sensitive to artistic reserve, are not always satisfied with highly reserved ending.

The story-teller should cultivate sensibility to story-building; it is the creative principle of story-telling. It is really surprising how lacking the beginner is in consciousness of structure. He should study structure until he can feel the tale making: the scene putting in, the people coming in, the motive revealing itself, the action starting, and going forward until it arrives at climax and solution, the whole winding up with happy prophecy of the far future.

Grasp especially the composition of the *action*. It is usually built on one of the following plans:

(a) The single line of sequence, as in Hans Andersen's "Princess on the Pea," or "The Sleeping Beauty," or "The Frog Prince;"

(b) The three-parallel line—what the first did, what the second did, what the third did,—as in "The Golden Pears" and in "Dummling;"

(c) The balanced antithetical plan, two contrasting courses of action placed side by side,

> what the beautiful, industrious child did
>
> what the ugly, idle child did,

as in "Mother Holle" or in "Diamonds and Toads."

(d) The cumulative plan, as in "Henny-Penny," "The Cat and the Mouse in the Malt House," "The House that Jack Built," "The Old Woman and her Pig." Do not miss the increase in interest and suspense.

Note in the three-parallel structure the climactic "thirdness" and its distinguishing characteristic; it is the youngest and the stupid third member of the family who turns out to be the cleverest and most favored of fortune; it is Dummling who marries the sweetest princess; it is the woodcutter's third daughter who proves considerate of the dumb animals, frees the castle of enchantment, and marries the prince.

Note, too, that the old-world story-tellers were sensitive to the dramatic effect of the contrasts in life. The miller's daughter, innocent victim of her father's ambition, sits down in despair to weep over an impossible task, and "at this moment the door opens and in comes a comical little dwarf" who with three magical whirrs of the spinning-wheel turn a roomful of straw into gold. It is the very day of her fifteenth birthday that the princess must take to explore the castle and come upon unsuspected spinning-wheel with which to prick her finger that the witch's prophecy may be fulfilled, but, as is the merry good luck of romance, it is on the last day of the hundred years that the prince goes hunting to spy, not deer, but the towers of the identical castle in which the Sleeping Beauty lies, inquires about it of everyone until he meets the very man who can tell him what "my father told me," and rides off to awaken the princess. It is always so in literature sound at heart, whether it be in a Shakespearean comedy, in which cottages appear in the forest in the nick of time as night is falling and lovely ladies and gallant knights are footsore and weary; or whether it be in simple fairy tale abounding in porridge pots, appearing when folks are on the brink of starvation and cooking like mad, "as if they would feed the whole world" at the magic words, "Little pot, cook," or in frogs popping out of near by wells in time to say, "Your wish shall be fulfilled, within a year you shall have a little child," or in small ovens and red apple-trees placed "conveniently low." The scholarly student of narrative or dramatic technique recognizes this as what he calls *comic relief* to offset the pathos of the situation; the student lacking this knowledge accepts with satisfaction the plausibleness of timely happening.

After this careful work read the story again for enriched appreciation of it. Now put the book away and go about your business.

By and by see whether you know the story. Let no mistrust born of book dependence and neglect of the constructive imagination daunt you. Boldly sketch in time and place, introduce the first characters, suggest the motive of the action, start the action, carry it forward to climax and solution, wind up the whole. Now criticise your product. Is it the thing you meant it to be? Thackeray tells us his characters and plots got out of his hands and finished themselves. Is it the tale as "'twas told to you," is it an improved version, is it a new story? One and all may be in place.

Some will feel that they have spoiled the story. They have bungled the structure through unskillful placing, or omission of necessary details. They have dulled life, dimmed beauty, obscured truth for lack of words. Well, there is no harm done as yet. These students, studying again the parts in which they failed, will appreciate now more thoroughly play and interplay of character, detail and course of action, vivid word. The cat in "The Bremen Town Musicians," they will note, is capitally described (in some accepted texts) as having a face that looked like "three days of rainy weather;" Snow-White and Rose-Red were "like the rose-bushes in their mother's garden;" they will not miss in "The Cat and the Mouse" the cat's sly description of the pot of fat and the apt names he gives his bogus godchildren. In this way the appropriate word or phrase will come to them easily.

The question often asked, "Am I to hold myself to the text?" is interesting. It applies of course only to artistic texts, not to formless source material. Some people contend that this destroys the spirit of story-telling, making the art mechanical instead of creative.

Story-telling is creative effort, never mere repetition of the letter. It is creative effort, whether you make live again something produced by another, or make live more abundantly by perfecting matter and form produced by another, or make new life. The question cannot be answered offhand. If it were true that the text form, the composition and diction, in which you found the story, were the perfect reflection of its life and that the story suffered no change in your comprehension of it, and that it were your intention to pass it on without modification or loss to the child, and that he could receive it without change in form, then the answer appears to follow: you are to be faithful to the text. In some cases the form in which the folk tale is found has suffered through translation, in others it may be intrinsically faulty; in many texts of "The Frog Prince," for example, the Iron John incident is too detached and very much out of perspective. The story-teller who can make it better should do so, or who feels prompted to give the children another product from old materials will use them, though the folklorists will forbid him to palm off his product as old-world lore. Any training in story-telling that does not give outlet and direction to such ability and to originality neglects an important obligation to the student. It is notable, by the way, that it is the student with the literary artist's instinct who is surest to "get" the style of any good original he may be reproducing. Proper simplification of standard texts and the question of adaptation to younger and older audiences will be considered later.

Are we not inconsistent in our attitude toward form in language? We profess to recognize reverently an intimate relation between the matter and the manner in the sculptor's, the painter's, the musician's art. But we constantly deny any integrity to language as a medium of expression. We do not, to be sure, attempt to tamper with the form the great poets gave their message. Indeed we "get" the verse running through the simple prose tale, although it is scarcely less artless than is the prose. But everyone because he can speak in words appears to feel competent to tell the prose body of the stories in "his own words." Now, every word in the folktale may not be so necessary to its thought as very minute details in Shakespeare's or even in Kipling's or Andersen's or Stockton's form are considered to his thought. But there is such a thing as folk-story style, easy, loose sentence liberally sprinkled with *and*s and *so*s, picture-making word, distinctive epithet, recurrent jingle, rhythmic swing. It is surprising how insensible students are to it. Yet it is due largely, no doubt, to the best of all causes, the belief that the story is to be given living form by the teller. Dull rote memorizing will not of course do this. The method of study set forth suggests how the story-teller may easily develop sensibility to folk-story style and easily train himself to "do," or "catch," it.

Let us not be afraid of a due regard for form. Right attention to form is not testimony to the worth of the superficial. The poet says, "The soul is form and doth the body make." Let us see to it that we make the language body of our story by clear reflection of its spirit.

The question of oral interpretation, or oral form, the more important aspect of form, while properly a matter to be settled by the student during the stage of preparation, is here more conveniently considered under the next head.

TELLING THE STORY

This is truly the stage of creation. No matter how familiar you made yourself with the story in the privacy of your studio, you will now find happening something surprising. The story will come to your own ears and stand revealed to your imagination with the joy of discovery. The truth is, it was made to be shared with another, and you hadn't it at all until you gave it away. What spontaneity rewards you! How you find yourself rising to the occasion—your own latent capabilities, the expanding possibilities in the story, the response of your audience!

Let us take up the topic, *telling the story*, under the practical heads:

(1) *Choosing or meeting story-telling time*;

(2) *The story-teller's part*;

(3) *Controlling canons of the story-teller's part*.

(1) *Choosing or meeting story-telling time.* "To everything," says Ecclesiastes, "there is a season and a time for every purpose under the heaven ... a time to weep and a time to laugh ... a time to keep silence and a time to speak."

Is there an ideal time for telling a story? Assuredly; at this time the story comes to the listener with more pleasure, or stronger appeal to the feelings. But the "pedagogical" story-teller, parent or teacher, must take care not to mistake suitable occasion. The error is not that the story-teller may have, like the Ancient Mariner, a tale of sin and virtue to tell to the soul that must hear it. To say that the story must not be narrowed to didactic purpose is not to exclude altogether the story that may work spiritual reformation. The trouble is that the story-teller sometimes precipitates irritation rather than reformation by untimeliness. The moment when the child is defiant or angry and the teacher or parent cross is not the psychological moment for such a story. It is at the turn in the tide of feeling that the story-teller may send into the wavering stream the saving grace of the tale.

There are times when the pupils are "on" for a mental frolic; these are the times for the play or "funny" stories. Sometimes, in order to quicken desirable response, the teacher or parent will judge it better to run counter to the mood of the children. She will sharpen the wits of dull children with a humorous story, or broaden the horizon of the narrowly matter-of-fact with a tale of adventure or of supernatural occurrence. Celebrations or memorials call out appropriate stories. The early Hebrew father took advantage of his sons' questions about the festivals celebrated in their midst to tell the great Bible story. The Christian Church sometimes narrates the lives of the saints to her children on feast days to inspire the heroism of holy living. Things observed in nature, and home and school circumstances, will suggest many stories. And when all has been said about special times, it remains true that almost any time in the wonder years of childhood is story time.

But the teacher may say, "Story-telling time means precisely eleven-fifteen on Tuesday morning; the individual teacher has nothing to say about it." The thing to do, then, is to induce the story-telling mood at eleven-fifteen Tuesday morning. What we should urge here between ourselves is the obligation to give place heartily at this time to the story. No matter how ill things may have gone and how cross we ourselves may have become, we must now let pleasurable anticipation take possession of the classroom.

(2) *The story-teller's part.* The rôle of story-teller is simple yet subtle, more easily shown than explained. The story-teller is recounter of a happening, real or fictitious, merry or pathetic, that because of its appeal to the imagination and sympathies has been given currency in language. To share with another the glimpse of life it gives the imagination, the feeling it arouses, the æsthetic satisfaction it yields, was man's reason for telling it. The story-teller's part, then, is so to employ and interpret the medium of currency as to free this force.

Beginning the story. The story-teller should begin the story with the air of having something interesting and enjoyable to tell. If the contents of the story had not been interesting, they would never have made a story; the story-teller may depend on this intrinsic interest. He should have also the air of leisure; story-telling is one of the social arts of leisure and pleasure; besides, stories record significant occurrences, which should be given the emphasis of time. His initial manner should give hint of the spirit of the particular story he is to tell. The first phrase, "There were five-and-twenty tin soldiers," sounds the playful martial spirit of Hans Andersen's "Brave Tin Soldier;" the story-teller echoes it in martial bearing and in martial swing and ring in his speech, in, of course, the playful manner of a story about a little toy soldier. Mother-love broods through the story of "The Wolf and the Seven Kids;" the story-teller suggests, in voice and eyes and fostering posture, its loving pride and anxiety. Should the story-teller begin in rather obvious make-believe-matter-of-fact style, his eyes hinting fun, the children will chuckle in delighted anticipation of a nonsense or a humorous story. The wholly impassive manner adopted by some story-tellers in telling "funny" stories to adult audiences will not do with children. The adult's enjoyment consists largely in his ability to remake as fun what the teller is representing as sober fact. Children, because of their lack of knowledge and experience, need more leading. Stories like "The Three Bears" correspond in spirit to nursery rhymes like "This little pig went to market;" they should be kept as childlike, mimetic, rhythmic, and playful. Southey gives the key to the spirit of "The Three Bears" in the setting. Every detail shows how well he caught the child-note: interest in wild animals, the bear a favorite; tendency to dramatic mimicry; response to rhythm; pleasure in possessions, this very complete "house of their own," kept by bears, delights the children. A hero story like "Jack the Giant Killer" calls for a bold spirit. "Snow-White and Rose-Red" sounds the domestic note: cheerful fireside group; mother reading from a "large book," children spinning, animals lying near. The setting here, though long, may easily be made attractive by the story-teller's own pleasure in every detail.

The characters also should be introduced with hint of their personality. "Snow-White and Rose-Red were as happy, as busy and cheerful," says the story-teller, showing cheerful pleasure in them, "as any two children in the world." "Snow-White," softening voice and eyes, "was more quiet and gentle; Rose-Red," adopting a livelier manner, "liked better to run about the fields and pick flowers and chase butterflies." "There was once a widow who had two daughters; one of them," says the story-teller, smiling in the pleasure goodness and beauty, whether physical or spiritual, always excite in us, "was pretty and industrious; the other," voice and face expressing disapproval of her, "was ugly and idle." "A certain man had a donkey," says the story-teller, with such suggestion of possibilities in the donkey evident in forward posture, in face and voice, that the listener at once suspects that, as Hans Andersen would put it, that donkey "became worth talking about."

The story-teller begins then, as both prophet and sibyl, telling yet, especially at this stage, not "giving it away." He must let the story reveal and the child discover; this is the joy of it.

Building out the story. Having laid the foundation upon which he is to build the happening, the story-teller should, as a rule, in building fashion pause. He then enters upon the action, carrying it forward, slowly or rapidly, according as its course demands, arousing suspense and increasing the interest in the outcome. How he does this will be suggested farther on. As the story proceeds he must of course treat character consistently. Sensibility to the nature of the particular character he is interpreting will enable him to voice and conduct it appropriately. Nothing more than suggestion is in place. The story-teller's fairy voice may be light and tinkling like silver bells, his witch made graphic through pointed, hag-like chin and fingers and stooped body, his fox smooth and sly, his wolf snarling, his giant, as said before, big-voiced and ponderous. He can hardly fail to catch the steely high voice and proud manner Hans Andersen intended for the vain but delightful Darning Needle.

After, as a rule, pausing to give effect to the climax of the action, the story-teller passes in many stories to a brief but clear explanation of enchantment, and winds up the whole happily, leaving the child supremely pleased.

(3) *Controlling canons of the story-teller's part.* Some of the chief canons governing the story-teller are *directness, spontaneity, graphicness, reserve, skill in the use of the voice, simplicity.*

Directness is the principle of immediateness, by virtue of which *story* and *listener* are brought into contact. It has its roots in the social and magnetic nature of the art. In its fullest sense it is comprehensive of all the other canons.

Directness concerns both the outer and the inner self of the story-teller.

The part played by the outer self is simple. Before beginning his story the story-teller should "go to" and "gather" his listeners. He does this by assuming the physical position and mental attitude of communicator. A person who has anything to tell another that he thinks will move or please him does not stand aloof. The story-teller should not stand aloof. He may place himself in front of his listeners, at such a point as will enable him to command all. Before beginning he will get the listening attention by invitation of posture and direct face to face look, or by the magnetic force of the story now animating his whole person. Some story-tellers then begin to address themselves to someone near by whom they feel to be the most responsive listener, or whom they wish to interest, then address a wider and wider circle until they are reaching everyone. Others project the story into the ears of someone in the middle of the group, making this the radiating point from which to grasp all.

The story-teller through his outer self must observe the principle of directness in another way. In looks and actions his external self must help to convey the spirit of the story: posture, facial expression, gesture, voice must not contradict but declare what the lips are saying. It is in recognition of the relation between the external self of the story-teller and his story that some story-tellers "make up," or put on appropriate costume. This has its power and charm. But for the "everydayness" of story-telling in home and school it is undesirable, unnecessary, and impracticable. What is necessary is something less troublesome but more important: such domination, or absorption, of the external self by the spirit of the story as will subdue it to the story-teller's use. This will help to induce the right feeling response. Feeling, as everyone knows, is "catching." Fun will call out fun; pathos, pathos; gladness at beauty, goodness, or truth, like joy. The whole being of the Ancient Mariner told his story. Simple stories do not demand emotional intensity, but the principle remains. The student will find it helpful to sit opposite Tadema's "Reading Homer," to get an idea of the recounter's abandon.

The principle of directness as it applies through the inner self of the story-teller is as easy to understand. The story-teller must not allow any intruding mental state or circumstance, any intruding "self," to come between the story and the listener. Such a self may be

(1) The diffident or embarrassed self of the self-conscious story-teller.

(2) The vain or affected self of the insincere story-teller.

(3) The weakening self of the patronizing story-teller.

(4) The non-seeing self of the non-spontaneous story-teller.

(5) The non-sensible, or non-artistic, self of the "sledge hammer" story-teller.

(6) The non-communicating self of the "acting" story-teller.

(7) The misinformed self of the lifeless story-teller.

(1) The self-conscious self is not hard to overcome. Diffidence arises from a false modesty, due to the story-teller's failure to realize his obligation to the child and to the story. His part now is not to occupy himself with mistrust of his own ability, but to bend all his energies to interpreting the story for the listener. Embarrassment may be due to natural shyness or to lack of ease in the art of story-telling. If due to the first, it should also disappear as the story-teller realizes his obligation; if to the second, time and practice will probably cure it. It is well to throw off embarrassment vigorously at the outset and plunge into the story; it is surprising how easy and complete will be the victory.

(2) Vain insincerity is a more serious intrusion. It shows itself usually in an affected manner and a false ring in the voice. The story-teller is not engaged in telling the story, but in exhibiting himself. The children will at once sense such a fraud. The pity is that they should ever have had the chance to do

so; it is often the beginning of insincerity in them. This story-teller also must strive to realize his important office.

(3) A patronizing story-teller is as great an obstruction. His manner is unctuous and "glawming." It dwarfs the listener, belittling him and undermining his frankness. Hear how the great queen did in Morris's tale:

> "Then she held him a little season on her weary and happy breast,
>
> And she told him of Sigmund and Volsung and the best sprung from the best;
>
> *She spake to the new-born baby as one who might understand."*

The spirit of the italicized words should be the story-teller's guide. Watch the child the first time he comes under the sway of the patronizing story-teller, how he eyes the babying smile meant to be engaging, how he holds aloof. The story-teller must trust the child and trust the story. He chooses the story for its suitability in arousing and directing the child's imagination, sympathies, or æsthetic sense. Having made the selection on this basis, his part now is to be, not officious meddler, no matter how well meaning, but communicator.

The patronizing story-teller is inclined to "thin out" the story. There is a proper kind of remaking allowable in telling a story or in fitting it to younger or older audiences. If too much is necessary, the story is probably not in any degree suitable; it might better be left until the children are older. There are for the meantime plenty of stories more nearly available. Some modes of simplification of the content allowable are: omission of details in description and omission of minor characters and incidents, in some cases to be added later; preparatory talk or explanation, reduced to its very lowest terms; conversation or explanation after the telling, to be followed soon by another telling. The form may be made easier by simplification of the complicated sentences or unchildlike modes of speech, by very sparing use of running explanation, by use of roundabout easier phrase to be replaced by the directly descriptive word.

The power and the glory for the listening child are more surely in the message as the *seer*, yourself or another story inventor, saw and delivered it, than in any garbled paraphrase of it, all that many attempting story-telling can manage. Their opportunity lies in the field of interpretation, unless they are genuinely engaged in changing the story or in themselves telling a different story or in truly artistic simplification. Have faith in the little child: in his sensibility to artistic fitness, in his intelligence, in his ready sympathy. Have faith in the story.

Best of all modes, the story may be simplified, not by making it over into something else, but by making it into itself through interpretation.

(4) Some story-tellers bring an uninformed self to the story. The root of their difficulty is failure to see and feel the child world. So important is the principle of insight that it will be taken up at length, under the heading *spontaneity*.

(5) A story-teller lacking in artistic sensibility does not discern the story as a form of art, though a naïve form. He intrudes between the story and the child what, for lack of a better term, the writer called a "sledge-hammer" self, or a didactic self. It resorts to pedagogical pounding, dealing largely in stress on words and in the falling inflection. It vainly attempts to force the story and the child into contact through the intellect, or sometimes the bugaboo of conscience, instead of by the open pathway made by freeing the spirit of the story.

One example, by the way, of the tendency to force the didactic note is the made over version of Southey's "Three Bears," in which the story begins with Silver Locks (the little wee woman of the older version is coming back) and makes much of her naughtiness, left in Southey's story to indirect playful condemnation. This puts her at once in the emphatic position, robbing the three bears of their rank, and the story and the children of the play spirit.

(6) The story-teller who confounds dramatization (not dramatic suggestion) with narration substitutes a detached exhibiting self for the story-teller's intimate, communicating self. He fails to tell the story. This also will be considered at length under another canon.

(7) Finally, an intruding self is the misinformed self of the lifeless story-teller. It makes story-telling nothing but colorless word-calling. It arises from a false psychology, resting on the assumption that the child's imaginative and emotional life differs in kind from the adult's (sound in so far as it condemns strain on the imagination and the emotions); a false ethics, mistrusting attention to oral form, or to beauty of speech; wrong habit in speech. Whatever its source, it prevents the contact of child and story.

The canon of directness, then, requires that both the outer and the inner self lend themselves to telling the story to the listener without obstruction.

Spontaneity is the canon of naturalness, by virtue of which the story has genuine life. It creates the illusion that the story-teller is spinning his tale from within out, its life having become part and parcel of his imaginative and emotional experience. It depends upon insight. The story-teller of childlike tales must "live with our children," as Froebel said; he must cultivate sensibility to the child's world, catch its spirit of play and happiness and activity, respect its serious moods, note its affectionate intimacy with animals, cats and dogs and hens and horses, respond to its humor, feel above all its emotional sincerity and simplicity. The child carries himself unaffectedly. It is easy to detect the story-teller who fails of insight into the child's world. He is either wholly insensible to its characteristics, or he grotesquely exaggerates everything. The first method leaves the child unmoved, the second undermines his sincerity.

The story-teller need not, however, be afraid to give full value to story materials: to idealize its people and happenings; to make its heroines frankly good and beautiful, its supernatural properties adequate, its "great huge bears" satisfyingly huge; to give its seven-leagued giants voice possibilities that will cause half-quaking, half-chuckling listeners to shake in their shoes in whole-hearted enjoyment; to make its porridge pots, that cooked or stopped the minute a certain good little girl said so, magical. Story art, like all art, idealizes its materials the moment it selects them; the story-teller in turn holds them up to view of the imagination. Nor need the adult story-teller be afraid of illumining the view more fully than might a child teller, by the light of the adult's richer knowledge and experience. No, the story-teller is not to impoverish nor dull the story; but he is to guard against giving the listener the impression of unsuccessful pretense at it, and against urging him to strained imagining and feeling. Until, alas, custom stales him to its false ring, a child condemns the unseeing story-teller, not recognizing him as kith nor kin.

To satisfy the canon of spontaneity, then, the story-teller must see and feel the tale he attempts to tell, that he may re-create its spirit.

By *graphicness* is meant vividness, by virtue of which the story is made plain to the imagination and quick to the feelings. It is secured by the various means of oral interpretation (to be considered under another heading), helped out by facial expression, and sometimes by gesture or by dramatic suggestion. It is governed by the imperative complementary canon of *reserve*. *Reserve* is the canon of artistic restraint; as applied here, it keeps story-telling the art of communicating, not allowing it to pass beyond the limits of dramatic suggestion into dramatization.

It is the greater degree of artistic reserve that divides story-telling sharply from dramatization and gives it its special magnetic charm and enduring strength. The essence of dramatization is sensible actualization, the essence of story-telling is imaginative suggestion. The story tells, yet leaves to the listener exhaustless discovery. At each re-telling the story allures the listener's imagination to catch added import. The listener maturing into the adult may penetrate a specific detail in the childlike allegory and uncover a symbol of everlasting life, eternal youth or truth or beauty, and having found it, he can never with listening exhaust the depths of it. Is it fanciful to conjecture whether it be some response to this imperishable integrity that urges children to demand the same tale over and over again? Psychology has discerned in them wiseacres learning the realities of life through play. Why not also through story?

Dramatic suggestion as an aid to language and subordinate to it is, however, in place. It was indulged in freely by primitive story-tellers. Children use it instinctively. Hint of happening, by show of action; or glimpse of character, by posture, facial expression, suggestion in tone, is sufficient. Such hint at once makes the situation or character plain to the imagination. The queen in Hans Andersen's "Princess on the Pea," for example, is well brought into the story by the story-teller's taking on a look of shrewdness, with perhaps shaking of the head, before he tells what the queen thinks of this "real" princess who presents herself thus bedraggled. In doing this the story-teller must preserve the appearance and intention of narration. As soon as some students of story-telling attempt dramatic suggestion they lose the listener and lapse into playing rather than telling. Even when dialogue or monologue demands a degree of impersonation the story-teller must keep in mind that it is for the purpose of *telling* the story to the listener. He *shows*, or *illustrates*, looking back to insure that the listener is following, or to make communication. After the story-teller's pantomime of surprise and delight at finding the shoes, in "The Elves and the Shoemaker," for example, he looks at his listeners to communicate his feeling to them and invite their corresponding emotion, then makes verbal communication to them.

Suggestive gesture may also be used to make language graphic. (Beginners often neglect to keep the hands free for gesture they may be impelled to use.) For the sake of the child we must recover, if we have lost it, the speaking face, animated body, and eloquent hand of our childhood. As the word gains in meaning, we resort to gesture more sparingly. Gesture should precede the word. Watch the unconscious child in his use of gesture; he tells with the hand and body before he tells with the word. Some beginners drop a gesture so quickly that they might as well have done without it, others sustain it too long. Gesture is used, as a rule, for one of two chief purposes, demonstration or appeal to the imagination or feelings. When the story-teller is using it to show shape or size or place, he does not need it any longer after he has done this. If he is using it to send the imagination of his listeners out or to appeal to their emotions, he must sustain it until it has accomplished its effect. Sometimes a quick strong gesture makes powerful appeal to the imagination; sometimes sustained gesture serves as aftermath, still telling to the imagination. Gesture must not appear detached from the story-teller, that is, put on from the outside; it should come from within, in the story-teller's effort to tell. It is helpful, too, to note that gesture partakes of the imitativeness of art,—thus we speak of *kingly* gesture, *commanding* gesture, *witchlike* gesture. When dealing with things that address themselves to the expanding imagination, gesture should be indefinite and broadly suggestive rather than definitive. Too prescriptive an indication of the size of the bears in "The Three Bears," for example, dwarfs for some generous imaginations the delightful hugeness of the great huge bear and the irresistible littleness of the little small wee bear. Free sweeping gesture is in place in the heroic legend.

Suggestive posture is another means of giving vividness. The story-teller might learn much from the painter and the sculptor about the eloquence of pose. The Pre-Raphaelite school of painting was no doubt guilty of extravagance, but in pose and facial expression it caught some of the secrets of artistic suggestion. We know how the sculptor, too, represents listening, or surprise, or courage. The sculptor is, of course, very much more dependent on posture than is the speaker. But posture should help the story-teller, just as do tone and quality and rate of voice. It will not do, for example, to settle back heavily in the seat while telling, "Out popped the gingerbread boy and—" It must not be forgotten, however, that pose also is under the imperative restriction of reserve; narration is not the static art of posing. Constant or violent change in posture, too, except in particular stories demanding it, is out of place; story-telling is the quiet if animated and graphic art of communication. Posture and facial expression, like gesture, should precede the word, prophesying of it, and sometimes be sustained during pause for effect.

Before leaving this canon, the story-teller should understand that graphicness should sometimes be veiled under a pervading elusiveness. Some stories should be wrapped about with the charm of impalpability; the mystery of them is the secret of their appeal. This is the atmosphere for the romantic fairy tale, like "The Sleeping Beauty," and for many of the legends and romances.

We are now ready to sum up the canon of graphicness. We have defined it as the dynamic principle of vividness by virtue of which the story is made plain to the imagination. It is secured by the supreme agency of speech, aided sometimes, in greater or less degree, by posture, gesture, facial expression, and dramatic suggestion. It is under the imperative restriction of the canon of reserve.

In an art defined as story-telling *the skillful use of the voice* is the chief technique to be mastered, and, alas, the least regarded. It is, however, gaining ground. Story-tellers are finding it increasingly reasonable to believe there is close connection between what is to be told and how it is told. While it is true that so strong is the vitality of the *what* that it will usually triumph in some degree over the *how*, this is no sound argument for abandoning it to that fate. It is also true, because of the social nature of language, that the listener will do much, no matter how dull the how, to inform and transform the what in the light of his own knowledge and experience. This is precisely in just measure what he is to do. But this argument also is weak.

Man tries to utter his meaning, to give sound to the sense of his thought. All students of words appear to agree to this as a primary creative principle. And in the utterance of language he employs instinctively what some story-tellers condemn as the "show" tricks of elocutionists: suggestive quality or pitch of voice; slow or rapid rate of speaking; grouping, inflection, and pause. Mastery of this instinctive use of speech in its fullness and perfection, as a means to an end, is what is meant by mastery of oral technique. Whatever the method of mastery, direct or indirect, surely the end should be granted.

It has taken many people a long time to convince themselves that the speaking voice is in need of proper exercise and training. They have expected too much of the speaker. The living person back of the speech, the personality, is the chief element in speech; without the speaker to utter his meaning, speech would be nothing but empty word mouthing. But they should give the speaker at least as much fair play as has the singer, training in the use of the voice. The set jaw, wrong coördination, the half-open throat, the closed glottis, or "voice box," the immobile lip (whose remedy, by the way, is not mouthing), the thick tongue,—all these, causing indistinctness, nasality, throatiness, are impediments to speech. So are throat or nasal or dental obstructions. So is incorrect breathing.

The nice art of enunciation and articulation is worth mastery. Phonics appears to some people like a science of very small things. It has not only an æsthetic value, but, if you must separate them, an intellectual value. Masters of enunciation and articulation give not only finish but richer meaning to language. This, again, is no doubt due to the lively connection between sound and sense. Open mouth and throat well to pronounce the vowels in *joy*, or *shine*, and confirm the truth of this; note the force of vowels, consonants, or aspirate pronounced accurately in *glisten, shimmering, hushed, croaked, scream, harsh*. It will be understood of course that the requirements of character suggestion may demand slurring, chopping off, drawling, and all sorts of speech vices; when in place they become virtues.

We are fond of using the expression "as natural as breathing." How many are breathing as nature would have them? The speaker should be past master of breathing: be able to expand the diaphragm and fill full and deep, to supplement this basal stock, as opening the mouth to enunciate a vowel or to speak a phrase gives easy, unobtrusive opportunity, to expend breath economically.

The story-teller should "find" his particular voice. To do this he may read or speak in his ordinary tone and note where it vibrates. This is his natural, or at least second-nature, voice, working basis for improvement; re-placing, purifying, strengthening, making flexible.

He should be able to place tone, to give it this or that quality, as the needs of interpretation may demand. He should be able to keep feeling out of the voice, and to speak with feeling without violating the principle of reserve.

Understanding, feeling, and æsthetic appreciation are rooted in the story-teller, to be sure, but they must be transmitted by the organs of voice. He will be delighted to find that the physical action of these organs, if easy and responsive, appears to deepen his own understanding and feeling and to send them in greater fullness to the listener.

One of the most important principles of oral technique is perspective, through which the central idea is kept dominant throughout the story. Proper application of this principle gives the whole story unity and increasing interest and point. To give the story perspective the story-teller employs grouping, pause, rate, pitch, and inflection. Space permits of nothing more than this mere enumeration of these means and of pointing out a very limited use of one or two. Beginners often err in grouping. In the story of "The Frog Prince," for example, they will say "there was a king," making this a more or less complete and leading idea, instead of "there was a king who had beautiful daughters;" at this point, moreover, by use of the complete falling inflection they destroy the subordinate relation of this idea to the succeeding one, "but the youngest was the most beautiful." Untrained speakers and badly trained readers overuse the falling inflection. Story-tellers will find it helpful to practice the sustained, or "forward pointing," voice. It is necessary to the proper building out of units of thought. The story-teller should "make," for example, the word picture with the voice, bit by bit, much as the painter does the line and color picture with the brush, each added detail going toward the whole.

Mastery of pause is important. In ordinary communication the story-teller, as does everyone else, uses pause a hundred times a day, but he is inclined at first to overlook its part in story-telling. He should learn to pause to make clear not only the divisions of single sentences, but of the whole story, its setting, action, resolution, and close. He should use it also to set off for dramatic emphasis or emotional effect significant or climactic circumstances, persons, or details of action. Pause is one of the simplest and most effective means of emphasis. Of course, like every other means of speech, it is sometimes best ignored.

This bare glance at speech technique shows us that the story-teller should have such command over the agencies of oral transmission as will enable him to convey the story fully to the listener. Let his point of departure be the effort to utter his meaning.

When telling stories to young children the story-teller may do more or less *"leading" of the feelings and the taste*, thus educating the child to respond to what is playful or brave or humorous or beautiful. If the story-teller will show pleasure in obedience, fun, good-nature, loveliness in nature or art, shape, for example, or color, or sound, or adaptability to use, the imitative listener will respond in like appreciation. Some beginners find it difficult to do this. Sometimes the source of the difficulty is bad habit in reading. This affects story-telling when the story has been prepared from the printed page. The student comes to the story-telling class with the habit formed of suppressing in his reading appreciation of excellence or of beauty. Two students talking together outside of class may do the natural thing; if describing beauty—loveliness of nature, human loveliness, goodness, heroism—they show pleasure in it by smiling lip and softly shining eye; "beauty," as Wordsworth has it, "makes them glad." But nine times out of ten the beginner in story-telling who has prepared the story from a book allows no appreciation of beauty to get into voice or self as he tells, for example, "In olden times, when wishing was having, there lived a king who had beautiful daughters, but the youngest was so lovely that even the sun himself, who has seen so much, marveled whenever he shone in her face." He is not of course to magnify this phrase unduly; he must keep it in proper perspective.

It is astonishing how imperfectly we talk and tell. As indicated before, words as they are uttered represent to the young listener, and, so lively is language, in great degree to the adult also, exactly what the speaker puts into them. If he utters *bright* dully, he contradicts truth; if he pronounces *loved* coldly, he robs it of the human warmth of itself; if he mumbles *lovely*, he dwarfs beauty. To correct wrong habit in speaking, the student of story-telling should cultivate sensibility to the feeling and æsthetic suggestions in language, and during the stage of apprenticeship be content to be conscious until more spontaneous appreciation shall relieve him of watchfulness.

To take another example, in the story of "The Hut in the Wood," beginners often fairly shout "night was coming on," "the owl hooted," "the trees rustled." The thing to be communicated here through the details is the emotional state of the girl. It is communicated by sympathetic interpretation: lowering of voice, with suggestion in it of the sounds heard, accompanied by shrinking in posture and dawning of fear in the face.

Leading is open to abuse. The more the language of the story tells on its face when interpreted so as to set free the associations bound up in it, the more the story-teller must trust it to carry its own effects.

The story-teller is governed most by the supreme canon of *simplicity*. His must be a peculiarly unelaborate, apparently artless art. In gesture and facial expression, in dramatic suggestion, in speech, his is that form or degree of the artistic manner that will carry to the listener the unaffected, frank, childlike kind of life with which the child story deals: *not intense in manner, not intellectual nor artificial in gesture, not pedantic nor studied in speech*—but *sincere and simple*.

THE CHILD'S PART IN STORY-TELLING

Let us tabulate some of the things the child naturally does as his part in story-telling. The table will be incomplete, but it may be suggestive. What is the child's part in story-telling?

(1) *It is listening.*

(2) *It is remaining silent.*

(3) *It is commenting.*

(4) *It is joining in.*

(5) *It is re-telling.*

(6) *It is partial re-telling.*

(7) *It is telling other stories.*

(8) *It is inventing stories.*

(9) *It is expressing sometimes story images in other media.*

(10) *It is sometimes playing the stories.*

(11) *It is growing by the power and grace of the story.*

(1) *It is listening.* Let us not underrate the child's quiet part as listener harkening to the story again and again to catch wider and deeper vision of it.

(2) *It is remaining silent.* When it is the silence of delight, be content; this is result enough. When it is the spiritual silence out of whose brooding may

be born reverent awe or insight into justice or cheerful good will or virile endeavor, bring all your wisdom to bear to decide whether you will help or hinder by leaving the child to himself, and in case of doubt give the story the benefit of it, trusting it to deliver its own message in due season.

(3) *It is commenting.* On the other hand, do not be unmindful of another opportunity. A child, like an adult, is inclined to talk some stories over; meet him halfway. Indeed, in some cases, lead the way; stimulate an inert class to talk over some of the more objective type of stories. It is your opportunity to get and clarify the child's point of view.

(4) *It is joining in.* We learn, from the snatches of story-telling history that have come down to us, that it was the custom of the audience to join in at the rhythmic repetitions, as people do at the chorus of a comic song. The children show the same tendency; encourage it. It not only pleases them, but it is an easy and natural beginning in reproduction. The child's dramatic sense prompts him to come in also when the story-teller reaches dialogue; encourage this also.

(5) *It is re-telling.* Rightly conducted, reproduction of stories is profitable for shaping the pupil's thought and language mode. But is the exercise rightly conducted? The children listen in breathless delight as the teacher tells the story; she demands it "back," the children struggle, interest flags, teacher and children toil on, and joy dies out in story and listener. This is too bad. Story-telling is a legitimate opportunity for unalloyed pleasure; the school is not too lavish of such times. What is the root of the trouble? It lies in one or more sources: the practice of requiring premature reproduction of some types of story not grasped by the children to the definite point of re-telling; the teacher's unreasonable or wrong standards of achievement; the pupil's lack of familiarity with the story, due to the teacher's tendency to turn reproduction into a test or task.

The tendency of the school to require immediate verbal reproduction of all stories is unwise utilitarianism. It is limiting the teacher's choice of stories undesirably. Feeling compelled to demand reproduction of every story, the teacher confines her choice to stories the children will take hold of easily. We can all testify that we have heard and been moved or delighted by recitals we could not reproduce; their purpose was to accomplish exactly what they did accomplish. The child is capable of responding in æsthetic pleasure or spiritual uplift to stories as yet beyond his re-telling. It is highly desirable that he be given the chance of contact with such material and that its seed be given time to root and flower. To urge him to immediate reproduction is to develop shallow glibness at the sacrifice of something finer. Under the compulsion of reproduction the teacher excludes, also, not only beautiful and spiritualizing stories, but long stories. Long stories are not desirable on the mere ground of length, but even this ground has its claim. The longer stories give sustained exercise to the imagination, and they give the story-teller ampler field to set forth character or action and to let the story yield fuller measure of delight. Short and long and longer and shorter are all in place. And not all need nor should be reproduced.

How much should the teacher expect when she asks pupils to tell back any stories they have heard only once, or at most twice? Exactly what the pupil gives, what he grasped. Many teachers are disturbed, however, by the meager "language training" afforded by this very brief re-telling. Why not let the stories, by reiteration of them on the teacher's part, impose their thought process and language mode on the forming habit of the child? This does not mean that reproduction must be verbatim repetition, nor that the children's individuality is to be suppressed. But what a mockery, especially in some quarters, is this prevalent idea in the schools that the child must not be familiarized with the language of the story, but that he should be compelled to "tell it in his own words." Alas, "his own words"! Would not familiarity with the story's language bring riches to the thought-starved and language-starved children of some unschooled parents, anxious that their children shall enjoy advantages denied to themselves? Would it not help in foreign sections?

(6) *It is partial re-telling*. Let the children come into possession of the story naturally and gradually. At each re-telling of it by yourself look for firmer and fuller reproduction. Help to keep the children's interest centered in the story, not so much by commenting patronizingly, "How well John told the story!" but rather by openly enjoying the story John is telling. Let language come, as it should, with the effort to express the thought. And do not interfere with composition by unnecessary questioning. Your first method of helping the pupils' reproduction might be by supplying omitted parts rather than by questioning analytically for them, as is so commonly done at present. (Questioning has of course its place: it serves to lift into consciousness the relations existing among the parts of the story.) Try co-operative telling: tell part yourself, then let a child or several in succession tell the next, helping if necessary but not anticipating, and perhaps finish the story yourself. The children will soon be able to manage more. Simple, artistic illustrative picture or blackboard sketches, showing in succession the main divisions of the story, will help to give it uninterrupted sequence. (When divisions are made either orally or pictorially, they should be true portions of the whole.) Presently the children will find themselves telling the whole of some stories without undue feeling of strain, and with great pleasure to themselves and their classmates.

Is it natural, by the way, to reproduce in the same company a story just heard? This is the common school practice. In an adult audience this would of course never be done except on the frank basis of practice in so doing or for some other accepted purpose. The children enjoy dwelling on the story. And they may practice, with the motive of telling the story at home. The teacher need not, therefore, strain at devices to make reproduction more natural, yet she might often take advantage of or contrive more natural occasion for it. The natural occasion is social intercourse and entertainment. There is space only to indicate one or two ways of securing this attractive natural motive. Sometimes let at least a day elapse before asking for the reproduction; you may then let the exercise be an opportunity to enjoy the story again. Tell the same story over and over (if it be a good one) yourself on appropriate occasions, and encourage the children to do the same thing. Let individuals, or groups, or classes, visit and exchange stories.

(7) The child's part, *telling similar stories* and (8) *inventing* stories, should go without saying. Do not neglect the opportunity offered by (8). If you reduce the class to workable groups at a time for this exercise, it should be practicable. Do not press prematurely the creative imagination, but do not neglect it. Give play to the natural working of a little child's fancy, the boy's or girl's, the youth's imagination. It is wise to follow the lead of the child here, then be at hand, not to deprive the child of the efficiency of independence and of the pleasure of making, but to help when necessary that his attempt may be encouragingly successful.

(9) *It is sometimes expressing story images in other media.* Here, again, the adult will do well to follow the lead of the child; of course of the most freely expressive child. The inert must be stimulated. Left to himself the child would not commit some of the excesses in sensible representation that adults impose upon children, though objective representation is natural to man at the childlike stage. It is not necessary that the child represent materially every set of language ideas. The teacher should not, on the other hand, stop natural attempt to represent even the more elusive kinds of ideas; there may be a budding Watts or Chase in her class, capable of picturing the highly fanciful and spiritual.

Keep the exercise growing. Its aim is to give constructive outlet to the child. The child's conception of the story, with expression of it and each rehearing, is growing. The practice of keeping a child's first attempts at expression in drawing or modeling or cutting or his attempts at any one stage too long about the classroom, before his eyes, is dwarfing. There is, of course, the other side to the question. To accept nothing as accomplishment is deadening to effort. It is possible, however, is it not, to meet the child on childlike standard of achievement, to acknowledge the day's accomplishment, yet without disheartening him, or even talking to him about the better things he will do, to keep *our* own faces turned toward the morrow?

(10) *It is playing the stories.* This, if not done with every story without discrimination, or without reference to the children's instinctive selective sense, if kept at least fairly spontaneous and progressive, is a form of constructivity heartily enjoyed by the children. It is wise here again to follow the child's lead. Let us understand, however, by this the lead of the majority of our most normal children and of the most gifted individuals. Many children meager in imagination, feeble in initiative, inadequate in execution, will need the strong lead of other children or of the teacher, qualified child seer from her experience with more favored children. Let her give to these from her abundance, becoming best playfellow and guide. But let her keep herself in the attitude of *playing with the children.*

Let us see how playing the story might develop. As soon as the story takes possession of the child he shows a tendency to enter into its persons and its action; to mimic the voices, to ape the manners, to do the doings. Give outlet to this; let the child take on and play out the life of the story, or yourself propose playing the story.

Do not, by the way, clutter up the child's direct outlet with staging and properties and stage terms. It destroys spontaneity and reality. Let the schoolroom be the place, and, as a rule, the school furnishings any necessary things, and the school children, in their ordinary clothes, the people. The delight of "dressing up" may sometimes be allowed; but a mere suggestion in costume, if it be something distinctive of the character impersonated, is all that is necessary; a gold paper crown, for example, will at once make a queen of any child. Why not with the little children talk simply and naturally: "Let us play" (not act nor dramatize) so and so. Who'll be so and so? I'll be so and so. Where will you have your home? And so on. Do not at the beginning *press* even this simple kind of planning; let the play develop with the playing of it. Help the children, however, gradually to gain in planning.

Playing has a tendency to make the form static; it is a mistake to let this happen too soon. Do not, as is the practice, stop telling the story yourself after the children have once played it. You will find that their intimate experience in playing it will bring a more pointed attention to the next hearing of it, and that their next playing will be richer in detail, or stronger in structure, or truer in characterization, or more appropriate in dialogue. Do not, of course, keep the children on one story either for playing or other form of reproduction until they weary of it.

Far from deploring, by the way, the child's crudities in dialogue, appreciate the opportunity to let him express himself and to develop his language sense. Keep the language way open to him. He will catch the force of your comment on how some character spoke, himself suggest to another pupil what the person the pupil is impersonating should say, note how you talk when you impersonate, or how you respond in dialogue with him.

Playing the stories is open to educational abuse by being turned into insincere show work. This results, too, in exclusion of pupils who do not excel. Keep playing the stories, at least for the little children, the spontaneous universal thing they make it—*play*. Their own selective sense guides them in assigning or assuming rôles. It is abused, also, by adult patronage. The teacher laughs at the children rather than with them, or laughs when the true child seer would be serious. The child thoroughly enjoys playing the stories, but this does not mean that he laughs constantly or at his own performance. Encourage him to catch the fun or humor of a situation or of a remark; enjoy the playing openly when it is merry, laugh and laugh heartily, but do not turn his genuine playing into a sham. Do not, on the other hand, take him too seriously; he does not always take himself so. In short, get the child's point of view here as elsewhere.

The "last's the best of all the game;" it is (11) *growing by the power and grace of the story*.

May the child nurtured on the wit and wisdom of the simple story simply told live happy ever after!

Thus we arrived at this place together, where the people were in the habit of spinning up the tow. It was an enforced custom with them that each in turn should relate some little tale, or history, and to tell the truth, not only the noble women, but also myself and my friend, found our entire pleasure in such stories, and we often used to stop old beggars and give them a trifle more for telling us them.

—JUCUNDUS JUCUNDISSIMUS, 1680.

STORIES

Now the children all draw near

'Tis the time a tale to hear.

THE FAIRY HORSESHOE

At midnight a long time ago an honest hard-working blacksmith heard someone in his shop hammering, hammering, hammering, for all the world like another blacksmith making a shoe. But the sound was very quick and light, more like tapping, tapping, tapping. And all the time, whoever it was was whistling the prettiest tune you ever heard, and singing between times:

"I'm a cunning blacksmith,

I can make a shoe,

Heat the iron,

Bend the iron,

Hammer it true—

Il y ho, il y hoo,

Il y ho, il y hoo—

I'm a cunning blacksmith,

I can make a shoe."

The blacksmith listened and thought, and listened and thought, and listened and thought. Then he sprang out of bed on tiptoe, crying softly, "I have it! I have it! It's one of the wee small people. I'll catch him if I can for good luck." The blacksmith needed some good luck. His work was to shoe the horse and shoe the colt and shoe the wild mare; and he did it well. But he hadn't enough to do, and so he was very poor.

Well, to go back, the blacksmith sprang out of bed on tiptoe. Then without making the least bit of noise in the world that ever was heard, he opened the door of his bedroom and looked all about the shop. He couldn't see sight nor light of anybody, but he heard the hammering, and whistling, and the singing between times:

"I'm a cunning blacksmith,

I can make a shoe,

Heat the iron,

Bend the iron,

Hammer it true—

Il y ho, il y hoo,

Il y ho, il y hoo—

I'm a cunning blacksmith,

I can make a shoe."

"It's very odd," said he, under his breath; "where can the wee small thing be!" All of a sudden, as he peered about more sharply, he spied it stuck in the girth of a white mare standing in the stall nearest the forge. The elfin smith was wearing a bit of an apron before him, and a tid of a nightcap on his head, and hammering away at a speck of a horseshoe.

"He'll bring me good luck, if I can only catch him," said the blacksmith so softly that his own ears could scarcely hear. And without making the least bit of noise in the world that ever was heard, he tiptoed up behind the wee small body, opened his hand, and—snatched him up, crying, "Ha, ha, I have you." With that he opened two fingers to take a look, when—out jumped the elf, crying, "Ho, ho, see me go," and away he did go like a streak of lightning.

But he left the wee bit horseshoe in the blacksmith's hand. And it did bring him good luck, so that ever after he had plenty to do. So many horses and colts and wild mares came to be shod that he had to build a larger shop with nine-and-seven stalls.

When the blacksmith died, he left the good luck fairy horseshoe to his sons, and they left it to their sons, and they left it to their sons; so that if they haven't lost it the blacksmith's great, great, great, great, great, great, great grandchildren have it yet.

—Angela M. Keyes

THE MOUSE AND THE SAUSAGE

Once upon a time a little mouse and a little sausage, who loved each other like sisters, decided to live together. They planned it so that every day one would go to walk in the fields, or to buy things in the town, and the other would stay at home to keep the house.

One day, when the little sausage had prepared cabbage for dinner, the little mouse, who had come back from town with a good appetite, enjoyed it so heartily that she exclaimed: "How delicious the cabbage is to-day, my dear!"

"Ah!" answered the little sausage, "that is because I popped myself into the pot while it was cooking."

On the next day, when it was her turn to prepare the meals, the little mouse said to herself: "Now I will do as much for my friend as she did for me; we shall have lentils for dinner, and I will jump into the pot while they are boiling." So she did, without stopping to think that a simple sausage can do some things not to be attempted by even the wisest mouse.

When the sausage came home, she found the house lonely and silent. She called again and again, "My little mouse! Mouse of my heart!" but no one answered. Then she went to look at the lentils boiling on the stove, and, alas! found within the pot her good little friend, who had perished for love of her. Poor mousie had stayed too long at her cookery, and when she tried to climb out of the pot, she had no longer the strength to do so.

The little sausage could never be consoled! That is why to-day, when you put one in the pan or on the gridiron, you will hear her weep and sigh, "M-my p-poor m-mouse! Ah, m-my p-poor m-mouse!"

—French Folk Tale

THE STORY OF THE LITTLE BOY AND THE LITTLE DOG

There was a little boy and there was a little dog. The two lived together and loved each other, and where one went the other followed.

Now, all of a sudden, the little boy and his nurse moved away to another city, far, far off. This puzzled the little boy so much that for once he forgot the little dog. When he remembered him, it was the middle of the night. But, for all that, he got up and waked his nurse to ask her where the little dog could be. The nurse rubbed her sleepy eyes and said,

"Sleep now, my lamb, and wait till day,

Thy little dog is on the way."

Then she closed her eyes and straightway fell fast asleep, and so there was nothing for the little boy to do but to fall asleep, too.

At break of day the little boy was at the window watching for the little dog. But alas! no little dog came. When the little boy asked his nurse what could be keeping the little dog, she said,

> "Be patient, my lamb, 'tis but peep of day,
>
> Thy little dog is on the way."

Well, the morning and the noon passed, and no little dog came. The little boy grieved so that he could neither eat nor play. At last when evening began to darken, and still no little dog came, and still the little boy watched at the window, the nurse put on her bonnet and shawl and went out to find the little lost dog.

It wasn't long before she was back with a dog that looked something like the dear lost one, but much thinner and quieter. When the little boy said so to his nurse, she said,

> "Yes, poor doggie! But he came a long way,
>
> Without bite or sup, a night and a day;
>
> Give him, my lamb, a bowl of warm milk,
>
> And soon you'll see him as sleek as silk."

The little boy ran and gave him the milk. When the little dog had lapped up the milk, he felt so much better that he licked the little boy's face, and the two frisked about the room.

But the little boy noticed that the little dog did not caper so merrily as he used to do. Indeed, the poor creature soon became quiet and sad again. And, although the little boy made his own legs go as fast as a windmill, he could not coax the little dog to run a race with him. He saw, too, that the little dog found it very hard to curl himself up on the hearthrug for a nap. And the next day the little dog was so wretched that he refused to eat.

"Poor, poor doggie, what ails you, whatever ails you?" cried the little boy. "You'll die if you do not eat." He lifted the dog tenderly into his lap, when—what should he feel on the stomach but a seam! "Nurse," he cried, "come quickly; something is stitched so tight around the poor dog's body he cannot eat nor breathe."

The nurse ran in with the scissors in her hand. And lo!

> With a nip and a snip, and snip and a nip,
>
> And a very loud pip!

out came the little boy's own little dog.

"Now I see through it all," cried the nurse. And what she saw was what had really happened.

While the little dog was on his way to the little boy, a dog-seller snatched him up and carried him into a shop. There he tried to change him into a French poodle by sewing him into a skin-tight black jacket with curly trimming. But by great good luck it was down the street past this very shop the nurse walked and spied the little dog peeping out to see how he might escape.

"Oh, I'll never forget thee again," cried the little boy. And he didn't. The two lived happy together ever after, and where one went the other followed.

—Angela M. Keyes

THE STORY OF THE TWO CAKES WHO LOVED EACH OTHER IN SILENCE

On the shop counter lay two gingerbread cakes. One was the shape of a man with a hat, the other of a maiden without a bonnet. Both their faces were on the side that was turned up, for they were to be looked at on that side, and not on the other. On the left the man wore a bitter almond—that was his heart. The maiden was honey-cake all over.

As they were only samples, they stayed on the counter a long time. And, at last, they fell in love with each other. But neither told the other, as should have been done, if anything was to come of it.

"He is a man and must speak first," thought she. But she was happy, for she knew he loved her.

His thoughts were far more extravagant; that is the way with men. He dreamed that he was a real street boy, and that he had four pennies of his own, and that he bought the sweet maiden and ate her up.

So they lay on the counter for weeks and weeks, and grew dry and hard.

But the thoughts of the maiden became ever more gentle and maidenly. "It is enough for me that I have lived on the same table with him," she said, and—crack! she broke in two.

"If she had only known of my love," thought he, "she would have kept together a little longer."

"And that is their story, and here they are, both of them," said the baker, for it was he who was telling the story. "They are remarkable for their curious history, and for their silent love, which never came to anything. There they are for you." So saying, he gave the man, who was yet whole, to Joanna, and the broken maiden to Knud.

But the children were so impressed with the story that they could only look at them, they could not eat them up just yet.

—Hans Christian Andersen

HOW THE ROOSTER BUILT A HOUSE OF HIS OWN

One spring day a young rooster set out on his two stout legs to build a house of his own. On he went, a long, long way, and a long, long way farther, and a long, long way farther than that.

Then he lifted up his voice and flapped his wings and crowed,

"Cock-a-doodle-doo.

I want a dame, I do."

At this out from somewhere stepped a bonny, wee white hen and fared along beside him.

On went the young rooster and the bonny, wee white hen a long, long way, and a long, long way farther, and a long, long way farther than that.

Then the young rooster lifted up his voice, flapped his wings, and crowed,

"Cock-a-doodle-doo,

There's room for a friend or two."

At this out from somewhere stepped a bearded goat, and a brindled cow, and a long-tailed horse, and a whiskered cat, and fared along beside him.

On went the young rooster, and the bonny, wee white hen, and the bearded goat, and the brindled cow, and the long-tailed horse, and the whiskered cat, a long, long way, and a long, long way farther, and a long, long way farther than that.

Then the young rooster lifted up his voice, flapped his wings, and crowed,

"Cock-a-doodle-doo,

My friends, will this place do?"

The bearded goat climbed up to browse on a rocky hill near by, and said it would. The brindled cow cropped the grass beside a running stream, and said it would. The long-tailed horse took a mouthful from a clump of wild oats, and said it would. The whiskered cat spied a field mouse scurrying into her hole, and said it would. The bonny, wee white hen had not spoken. The rooster looked about for her, so did the bearded goat, and the brindled cow, and the long-tailed horse, and the whiskered cat, but she was nowhere to be seen.

The young rooster lifted up his voice, flapped his wings, and crowed,

> "Cock-a-doodle-doo,
>
> Dame Hen, now where are you?"
>
> "Cut-cut-cut-cut-cadah-cut,
>
> Cut-cut-cut-cut-cadah-cut!"

cried the bonny, wee white hen, running out to tell him of an egg she had laid in the long soft hay.

"Well done," cried Father Rooster, looking very proud of her; "our peeping chicks will soon be out of the shell."

So then they all knew the place would do, and they set about building the house of their own. The long-tailed horse cut down a tree for wood with his strong teeth, the bearded goat rubbed the edges smooth with his horns, the brindled cow carried the beams on her broad back and stood them up in place with her forelegs, the whiskered cat sprang up and down the beams and nailed them together, the young rooster gave the orders to everyone, and when the house was done the bonny, wee white hen swept it clean as a new pin.

Then they all moved in. And there they lived in this house of their own for a year and a day, and a year and a day, and a great many more, as happy as bees in clover.

And the young rooster was cock of the walk.

—Angela M. Keyes

THUMBELINA

(Arranged as a continued story)

How She Came to the Woman

Once a woman wished she had a very little child, but she did not know where to get one. So she went to an old witch and said, "I wish I had a very little child. Can you tell me where I might get one?"

"Oh, that I can easily," said the old witch. "Here is a barleycorn for you. It is not the kind that grows in everyone's field and the chickens eat. Put it into a flower pot, and you shall see what you shall see."

"Thank you," said the woman, and she gave the witch twelve shillings, for that was the price of the barleycorn.

Well, the woman planted the barleycorn. And immediately there grew up a great handsome flower. It was like a tulip, but the petals were tightly closed as if it were still a bud.

"What a beautiful flower," cried the woman, and she kissed its yellow and red leaves. "Pop," the flower opened. It was a real tulip, but in the middle, there upon the green velvet stamens sat a tiny maiden, lovely as a fairy, and only half a thumb's height. So her mother called her Thumbelina.

And that is how she got her.

THUMBELINA

How She is Carried Off by the Toad

One night as Thumbelina lay sleeping in her pretty walnut-shell cradle, there came creeping through the open window an old Toad. He hopped straight down the table where Thumbelina lay.

"Ah, she would make a lovely wife for my son," said he. So he picked up the cradle with Thumbelina in it, and hopped through the window and down the garden to the brook. Here he lived with his son.

"What do you say to her for your bride, my son?" said he.

"Croak! croak! brek-kek-kek!" was all the son could say.

"Hush! Don't speak so loudly, or she will awake," whispered the old Toad. "She might run away from us, for she is as light as swan's down. We will put her out in the brook on one of the broad lily leaves; that will be just like an island to her, and she won't be able to get away. Then we'll go and get the best room in the marsh in order, where you are to live and keep house together."

So they swam out with her, and when they came to a broad lily leaf lifted her out of the cradle very gently without waking her, and swam back with it, because they intended to place it in the bridal room.

Well, when Thumbelina woke and saw where she was she began to cry bitterly, for there was water on every side of the great leaf and she could not get to land at all. The little fishes swimming below stuck their heads out of the water to see what was the matter. And when they saw Thumbelina they thought her so pretty that they drew in their heads and put them together under the water, and nibbled away at the stem until the leaf was free. Then away sailed Thumbelina, far off from the ridiculous toad and his son who could only say, "Croak, croak, brek-kek-kek."

THUMBELINA

HOW SHE GOT TO LAND

Thumbelina sailed by many cities, and the little birds who sat in the bushes saw her, and said, "What a lovely little girl!" A white butterfly fluttered round her and at last alighted on the leaf with her. Thumbelina was glad of his company; she took her girdle and tied one end of it around the butterfly and the other to the leaf. On she went, faster than ever now.

Soon there came a big May-bug flying toward her. When he saw her he thought her so pretty he clasped his claws round her waist, and flew with her up into a tree.

Mercy! how frightened poor little Thumbelina was! But the May-bug did her no harm. He seated himself with her upon the biggest green leaf of the tree, gave her the sweet part of the flowers to eat, and told her she was lovely, although she did not look a bit like a May-bug.

When the other May-bugs who lived in the tree heard of it, they all came to pay a visit. They looked at Thumbelina, and one said, "Why, she hasn't more than two legs; how very odd that is!"

"And she hasn't any feelers!" cried another.

"How squeezed she is at the waist—fie! How ugly she is!" said all the lady May-bugs.

So at last the May-bug who had carried her off thought so, too, although she was really very pretty; and he flew down with her from the tree and set her on a daisy and left her there.

But, anyway, she was on land again; that was something.

THUMBELINA

HOW SHE GOES TO LIVE WITH THE FIELD-MOUSE

The whole summer through Thumbelina lived quite alone in the great wood. She wove herself a bed out of blades of grass, and hung it up under a shamrock to be sheltered from the rain. She scooped the honey out of the flowers for food, and she drank the dew that stood every morning on the leaves. So summer and autumn passed.

Now came the winter, the long cold winter. All the sweet birds who used to sing to her flew away. The trees and flowers lost their leaves. The great shamrock she lived under shriveled up, and left her shivering. She tried to wrap herself in a dry leaf, but that tore in the middle. Soon it began to snow. Every snowflake that fell on her was like a whole shovelful thrown on us, for we are tall and she was only an inch high. Poor little Thumbelina! she was nearly frozen!

She wandered out of the wood into a withered cornfield. The corn had gone long ago; nothing but dry stubble stood up out of the frozen ground. But it was like a great forest for Thumbelina to be lost in. How she trembled with the cold!

After some time she came to a field-mouse's home. It was in a little hole under the corn stubble, warm and cosy. There was a kitchen in it and a pantry filled with corn. Little Thumbelina stood at the door just like a poor beggar girl and begged for a little bit of barleycorn. "I haven't eaten a crumb in two days," she cried pitifully.

"You poor little creature," said the kind field-mouse, "come into my warm kitchen and eat as much as you wish." And when Thumbelina came in, the field-mouse liked her so well that she said, "If you wish you may stay with me all winter, but you must keep my room clean and neat, and tell me little stories, for I am very fond of them."

So Thumbelina did, and had a very good time of it.

THUMBELINA

HOW SHE MEETS THE MOLE

One day when Thumbelina had tidied the house and made it look as neat as a new pin, she sat down to chat with the field-mouse.

"My dear," said the field-mouse, "we shall soon have a visit from my neighbor, the mole. He comes to see me once a week. Do you know, he would make you a good husband. He is rich. He lives in a much larger house than mine, and wears beautiful black velvet fur. When he comes you must tell him the prettiest stories you know."

And, sure enough, the mole came to see them, dressed in his black velvet fur. Thumbelina did not care for him at all. He talked about nothing but himself. He told how rich he was and how large his rooms were, twenty times larger than the field-mouse's, and he said he didn't like the sun and flowers, just because he had never seen them.

"How can you talk so!" cried Thumbelina, indignantly.

"Sing us one of your sweet songs, Thumbelina, my dear," said the field-mouse.

So Thumbelina had to sing. She sang, "Ladybug, fly away." She sang it so sweetly that the mole fell in love with her. But he did not tell her so yet. As for her, she was glad when his visit was over.

THUMBELINA

How She Takes Care of the Swallow

Well, the mole had dug a long passage through the earth from his house to the field-mouse's, and he told Thumbelina and the field-mouse they might walk in the passage whenever they chose.

"Don't be afraid of the dead bird lying there," said he; "come with me and I'll show you where it is." He led the way with a bit of rotted wood in his mouth to light up the long dark passage. When he came to the place, he thrust his broad nose through the ceiling to make a hole so that the daylight might shine down. And there in the middle of the floor lay a dead swallow, with his beautiful wings pressed close against his sides and his feet and head drawn in under the feathers. The poor thing looked as if he had died of cold.

Thumbelina was very sorry for him, but the mole gave the bird a push with his crooked legs and said, "Now he can't pipe any more. I'm glad I was not born a bird, and that none of my children can ever be birds. A bird can do nothing but say 'tweet tweet' in summer and starve in winter."

"Yes, indeed," cried the field-mouse, "you may well say you are better off to be a mole. You are clever, you can build and make underground passages where you may keep snug and warm in the winter. Of what use is all this 'tweet tweet' to a bird when the frost comes?"

But Thumbelina did not agree with them at all. When they turned their backs on the bird she bent down, gently moved the feathers aside, and kissed him on the closed eyes.

"Perhaps," she thought, "it was this very bird that sang so sweetly to me in the wood. He did far more for me than the mole does. How much pleasure he gave me, the dear, beautiful bird!"

The mole now closed up the hole and escorted the ladies home.

But that night Thumbelina could not sleep for thinking of the dead bird. So she got out of her bed and wove a soft blanket of hay. She carried this out into the dark passage and spread it over the poor bird. As she did so she laid her hand on the bird's heart. It was beating! He was not dead at all! only numb with cold.

When he grew warm through and through he opened his eyes and looked at Thumbelina. At first she trembled, she was so frightened, for the bird was very large to her, who was only an inch in height. But she was too kind to run away from him.

"Thank you, pretty child," said the sick swallow in a weak voice. "Now that I am warm I shall get strong again and be able to fly on my way."

"Oh, stay where you are," said Thumbelina, "it is so cold outside. It snows and freezes. Stay in your warm bed and I will nurse you."

She brought the swallow water in the petal of a flower. When he had drunk he told her all about himself. He had set out for the south, the warm countries, with the other swallows; but as he flew he caught one of his wings in a thorn bush and tore it. After this he could not fly so fast as the others, so the winter overtook him and he could not stand the cold. It benumbed him so that he fell to the ground. He could remember nothing more after this, until he opened his eyes and found Thumbelina at his side.

The whole winter Thumbelina nursed the swallow. And when the spring came and the sun was warm, she opened the hole in the ceiling and let the sunshine pour in on him.

"I am strong enough now to fly out into the sunshine," said the swallow. "Sit on my back and let us fly far into the green wood."

But Thumbelina would not do this; she knew that the old field-mouse would be lonely without her.

"No, I cannot," said she.

"Farewell then, you pretty, good child," said the swallow, and he flew off into the sunshine. Thumbelina looked after him, and the tears came into her eyes, she was so sorry to part with him.

"Tweet-tweet," he sang, as she lost sight of him in the green wood.

THUMBELINA

How She is Helped by the Swallow

"My dear," said the field-mouse one day after the mole had paid her a visit, "the mole has asked me to give you to him for his wife. You are very fortunate, a poor child like you. You must be ready to marry him as soon as possible. Set to work at once on your wedding-dress."

So Thumbelina had to turn the spindle to make herself not only a wedding-dress but plenty of wool and linen, for the field-mouse said she would not have her go to the mole empty-handed, as if she were a beggar-girl. And the mole himself hired four spiders to weave her a beautiful cobweb veil. And every evening he paid her a visit, and said they must be married as soon as the summer was over.

Poor Thumbelina did not know what to do. She did not wish to marry the mole, and live under the ground, where the sun never shone. The first thing every morning and the last every evening, she crept outdoors, and when the wind blew the corn leaves apart, she looked up at the sky and wished the swallow would come to her. But he did not.

When autumn came, Thumbelina had everything ready.

"Only four weeks more for the wedding," cried the mole.

But when he had gone home Thumbelina wept and said she could not marry the ugly mole, who talked about nothing but himself.

"Nonsense!" said the field-mouse, "don't be obstinate, or I'll bite you with my sharp teeth. The Queen herself has not such black velvet fur. And his kitchen and cellar are full. Be thankful for your good fortune."

Well, the wedding day arrived. The mole, dressed in his best black velvet, came to fetch Thumbelina to his house.

"Farewell, thou bright sun!" she cried, running out of the house a little way. "Farewell," she cried, twining her arms around a little red flower still blooming there; "say farewell to the little swallow for me, if you see him again."

"Tweet-tweet! tweet-tweet!" suddenly sounded over her head. She looked up; it was the little swallow, just flying by. He stopped when he saw Thumbelina, he was so glad. And Thumbelina told him how she was to marry the mole, and live deep under the earth, where the sun never shone. She could not help weeping as she told of it.

"Come with me," said the swallow, "I am on my way far off to the warm countries. Sit on my back, and we will fly from the ugly mole and his dark room. Only fly with me, you dear little Thumbelina, who were so good to me when I lay frozen in the dark passage."

"Yes," cried Thumbelina, "I will go with you." And she seated herself on the bird's back, and bound her girdle to one of his strongest feathers. Then the swallow flew up into the air and away over forest and sea and great high mountains, where the snow always lies, and on, on, on to the beautiful warm countries.

THUMBELINA

What Became of Her at Last

In the warm countries the sun shone so bright that in the ditches and on the hedges grew big juicy blue and green grapes, lemons and oranges hung in the woods, and the loveliest children ran about the roads chasing gorgeous butterflies. The swallow flew on until he came to a great palace with dazzling white marble pillars.

"My house is at the top of one of those pillars," said he, "but it is not good enough for you. It is not yet so well furnished as I should like it to be if you were to live in it. Pick out one of the splendid flowers you see down there, and I will set you down in it."

"That will be a beautiful home," cried Thumbelina, and clapped her hands. She chose a great white flower. The swallow flew down with her and set her on one of the broad leaves. What was Thumbelina's surprise? There in the flower sat a little man, shining white, with a tiny gold crown on his head, and bright wings on his shoulders; and he wasn't a bit bigger than Thumbelina herself.

"How handsome he is!" whispered she to the swallow.

"That is the king of all the flowers," whispered the swallow back to her.

The little king was afraid of the big swallow, but he liked Thumbelina the minute he saw her. She was the prettiest maiden he had ever laid eyes on. Instantly he took off his golden crown and put it on her head, asked her name, and begged her to be his wife and queen of all the flowers.

Now of course such a husband was much better than the toad's son who could say nothing from morning till night but "Croak, croak, brek-kek-brek;" and the field-mouse's neighbor, the mole, who could do nothing from morning till night but talk of himself. So Thumbelina said "Yes," with a right good will, to the charming Prince.

And out of every flower came a lady or lord, lovely to behold, and each brought Thumbelina a wedding present. But the best gift was a pair of beautiful wings that had once belonged to a great white fly. When these had been fastened on her by one of the lovely ladies, Thumbelina could fly from flower to flower, and visit everyone in her kingdom.

It was a joyful wedding. The little swallow sat above them in the nest,—he was to sing the marriage-song. And although his heart was sad to lose Thumbelina, he sang it sweetly.

So that is the end, and Thumbelina lived happy ever after.

—HANS CHRISTIAN ANDERSEN

A VISIT FROM AN ELF

One evening, as a farmer was crossing a field to his home, what should he see sitting on a stone in the middle of it but a tiny creature! The little thing looked something like a very, very, very small, teeny, weeny, tiny little child. And it was blue and shivering with cold. The farmer saw that it must be an elf.

He knew it would bring him good luck to be kind to it. Besides, he pitied it from his heart. So he took it home and placed it on a stool by the hearth, and fed it with sweet milk. Soon the bantling was warm and lively. He capered and sprang about the kitchen merrier than a cricket, and twice as light-footed.

Well, he didn't go the next day nor the next nor the next. He stayed for many days. A curious thing about him was that he never spoke. But that did not matter, for he kept the farmer and the farmer's wife laughing at his tricks.

He and they had many a play together. Sometimes, when the farmer's wife was not looking, he would creep into the keyhole. Then the farmer would call out, "Find him, wife."

At this the farmer's wife would search all about the kitchen, under the chairs, in the closet, behind the wood box, even in the clock case. But she could not find him. Then she would cry out, "Where are you, Tinykins?"

The farmer would chuckle and hee-haw, and slap his knee, and wink, and say,

> "He's neither in,
>
> And he's neither out;
>
> He's where something goes in
>
> When the light goes out."

Quick as the crow flies before the farmer's empty gun the farmer's wife would guess, "You're in the keyhole, Tinykins, you rogue, come out."

And out he would pop in high glee.

The way he went was as strange as the way he came. I'll tell you about it

One evening as the little fellow was frisking about the farm kitchen, a shrill voice from the farmyard called three times, "Tolman Grig! Tolman Grig! Tolman Grig!"

"Ho! ho! ho! My daddy is come," cried the elf, springing up and speaking for the first time.

With that, off he flew through the keyhole.

That was the last the farmer or his wife ever saw of him. But forever after they were happy and prosperous.

—Angela M. Keyes

HOW THE CAT GOT ALL THE GRAIN

Once upon a time a Cat and a Parrot owned a field together. One day the Cat said to the Parrot, "Come, friend, 'tis time to till the field."

Said the Parrot, "I can't come now, because I am whetting my bill on the branch of a mango-tree."

So the Cat went alone and plowed the field. When it was plowed the Cat went again to the Parrot and said, "Come, friend, let us sow the corn."

Said the Parrot, "I can't come now, because I am whetting my bill on the branch of a mango-tree."

So the Cat went alone and sowed the corn. The corn took root, and sprouted, and put forth the blade, and the ear, and the ripe corn in the ear. Then the Cat went again to the Parrot and said, "Come, friend, let us go and gather in the harvest."

Said the Parrot, "I can't come now, because I am whetting my bill on the branch of a mango-tree."

So the Cat went alone and gathered in the harvest. She put it away in barns and made ready for the threshing. Then she went again to the Parrot and said, "Come, friend, let us winnow the grain from the chaff."

Said the Parrot, "I can't come now, because I am whetting my bill on the branch of a mango-tree."

So the Cat went alone and winnowed the grain from the chaff. Then she went again to the Parrot and said, "Come, friend, the grain is all winnowed and sifted. Come and let us divide it between us."

"I will," shrieked the Parrot so loudly that he lost his balance, fell from the branch of the mango-tree, and cracked open his poll. That put an end to him. So the Cat had all the grain for herself.

—EASTERN FOLK TALE

THE TABLE AND THE CHAIR

Said the Table to the Chair,
"You can hardly be aware
How I suffer from the heat
And from chilblains on my feet.

If we took a little walk,
We might have a little talk;
Pray let us take the air,"
Said the Table to the Chair.

Said the Chair unto the Table,
"Now you *know* we are not able;
How foolishly you talk,
When you know we *cannot* walk!"
Said the Table, with a sigh,
"It can do no harm to try,
I've as many legs as you,
Why can't we walk on two?"

So they both went slowly down
And walked about the town
With a cheerful bumpy sound
As they toddled round and round;
And all the people cried,

As they hastened to their side,
"See! the Table and the Chair
Have come out to take the air!"

But in going down an alley
To a castle in a valley,
They completely lost their way
And wandered all the day;
Till, to see them safely back,
They paid a Ducky-quack,
And a Beetle and a Mouse
Who took them to their house.

Then they whispered to each other,
"O delightful little brother,
What a lovely walk we've taken!
Let us dine on beans and bacon."
So the Ducky and the leetle
Browny-Mousy and the Beetle
Dined and danced upon their heads
Till they toddled to their beds.

—EDWARD LEAR

THE WONDERFUL SHIP

"Once upon a time," said the stork, "and a very good time it was, there was a ship, a wonderful ship that could sail on land, dry land."

"Oh!" said the chicks.

"I know what I tell,"
Cried the stork,
"I know it well, very well,

I saw it with my own eyes."

"This wonderful ship went on legs," said the stork. "Long legs."

"Oh!" said the chicks and the ducklings.

> "I know what I tell,
>
> I know what I tell,"
>
> Shouted the stork,
>
> "I know it well, very well,
>
> I saw it with my own eyes."

"It had a head, and a neck that came down and went up like a hook," said the stork, "a big hook."

"Oh!" said the chicks and the ducklings and the little turkeys.

> "I know what I tell,
>
> I know what I tell,"
>
> Shrieked the stork,
>
> "I know it well, very well,
>
> I saw it with my own eyes."

"It had a hump on its back," said the stork, "a hump or two."

"Oh!" said the chicks and the ducklings and the little turkeys and the goslings.

> "I know what I tell,
>
> I know what I tell,"
>
> Cried the stork,
>
> "I know it well, very well,
>
> I saw it with my own eyes."

"It was—alive!" said the stork, opening his eyes and his mouth up so high that he could hardly get them down again.

"Ah, it wasn't a real ship at all," whispered the chicks to the ducklings, and they whispered it to the little turkeys, and they whispered it to the goslings.

"It was a camel," said the stork.

"What's that?" asked the chicks, the ducklings, the little turkeys, and the goslings. And they crowded around him.

"He's called the ship of the desert," said the stork. And he drew back to see what they thought of it.

"Why?" asked the chicks, the ducklings, the little turkeys, and the goslings.

"Ask your teacher," said he, flying off to his nest in the chimney top;

> "I must attend to my babies.
>
> Go to school;
>
> If you don't,
>
> You'll turn out geese and gabies."

At this minute, by great good luck, they heard Nan say to Ned, her brother, "Let's play school. I'll be the teacher." So they went to school.

And by great good luck Ned's lesson was about camels. "I'm not at all surprised," whispered the smallest chick to the biggest gosling; "I found a four-leaf clover in the grass this morning. I knew then we should have good luck."

They listened with all their might to the lesson, and when they found it too hard they stopped listening to talk it over. This was pretty often. So when they went home they knew as much about camels as the stork does, and maybe as much as you know.

—Angela M. Keyes

THE CLEVER GEESE

A long, long time ago when there were more foxes' dens than cats' cradles, there lived a very sly fox. Every evening this sly fox sneaked up through the tall grass and weeds and around the tree-trunks, pounced upon a plump young goose, and carried it off to his den.

First, he had one hidden away, then two, then three, then four, then five, then six, and by and by as many more.

Well, when he had a round dozen, he called them before him in a circle, fixed them with his bold sharp eyes, and said, "My dumplings, prepare to die. At moonlight, to-night, I dine on young goose."

"You'll surely give us time to say good-by," cried the poor simpletons, who suddenly turned clever to save their necks. "We have become the dearest of friends."

"With all my heart," said the fox, with a bow. "Take as much time as you like, my dainties, for the sweet parting." And off he went.

One silly goose began to giggle at their cleverness before he was out of earshot. But her sisters ran at her and pecked her into silence. They laughed with their eyes only, and so long as the fox kept walking away and not looking back that was perfectly safe.

Well, at moonlight, sure enough, the fox came home to dine. And at once the geese began to say good-by.

"Ga-ga-ga-ga-ga-" said one. And when he stopped for breath, "Ga-ga-ga-ga-" said another. And, when he stopped, another took it up. And after that, another and another.

So, for all I know, they are at it still. The fox has not yet dined, and the geese are alive and gabbling, though, as the story says at the beginning, it all happened a very long time ago, before any of us were born.

—Angela M. Keyes

THE HAPPY PRINCE

(Especially suitable in winter season)

High above the city, on a tall column, stood the statue of the Happy Prince. He was gilded all over with thin leaves of fine gold, for eyes he had two bright sapphires, and a large red ruby glowed on his sword-hilt.

"Why can't you be like the Happy Prince?" asked a mother of her little boy who was crying for the moon. "The Happy Prince never dreams of crying for anything."

"I am glad there is some one in the world who is quite happy," muttered a disappointed man as he gazed at the wonderful statue.

"He looks just like an angel," said the Orphan Children, as they came out of the cathedral.

"How do you know?" said the Mathematical Master, "you have never seen one."

"Ah! but we have, in our dreams," answered the children; and the Mathematical Master frowned and looked very severe, for he did not approve of dreaming.

One night there flew over the city a little Swallow. His friends had gone away to Egypt six weeks before, but he had stayed behind with the beautiful Reed. He had seen her early in the spring as he was flying down the river after a big yellow moth, and had stopped to talk to her.

"Shall I love you?" said he. "Shall I love you?" And the Reed made him a low bow. So he flew round and round her, touching the water with his wings, and making silver ripples. This lasted through the summer.

Then, when the autumn came, the other swallows all flew away. After they had gone he felt lonely.

"I am off to the Pyramids," said he to the Reed. "Good-by!" and he flew after them.

All day long he flew, and at night-time he arrived at the city. "Where shall I put up?" he said; "I hope the town has made preparations."

Then he saw the statue on the tall column.

"I will put up there," he cried; "it is a high place with plenty of fresh air." So he alighted just between the feet of the Happy Prince.

"I have a golden bedroom," he said softly to himself as he looked round and prepared to go to sleep; but as he was putting his head under his wing a large drop of water fell on him. "What a curious thing!" he cried; "there is not a single cloud in the sky, the stars are quite clear and bright, and yet it is raining. The climate in the north of Europe is really dreadful."

Then another drop fell.

"What is the use of a statue if it cannot keep the rain off?" he said; "I must look for a good chimney-pot," and he made up his mind to fly away.

But before he had opened his wings, a third drop fell, and he looked up and saw—Ah! what did he see?

The eyes of the Happy Prince were filled with tears, and tears were running down his golden cheeks. His face was so beautiful in the moonlight that the little Swallow was filled with pity.

"Who are you?" he said.

"I am the Happy Prince."

"Why are you weeping then?" asked the Swallow. "You have quite drenched me."

"When I was alive and had a heart to feel," answered the statue, "I lived in a palace. In the daytime I played with my companions in the garden, and in the evening I led the dance in the Great Hall. Round the garden ran a very lofty wall, but I never cared to ask what lay beyond it. My courtiers called me the Happy Prince. So I lived and died. And now that I am dead they have set me up here so high that I can see all the ugliness and all the misery of my city, and though my heart is made of lead, yet I cannot choose but weep."

"What! is he not solid gold?" said the Swallow to himself. He was too polite to make any personal remarks out loud.

"Far away," continued the statue, "far away in a little street there is a poor house. One of the windows is open, and through it I can see a woman seated at a table. Her face is thin and worn, and she has coarse, red hands, all pricked by the needle, for she is a seamstress. She is embroidering flowers on a satin gown for the loveliest of the queen's maids-of-honor to wear at the next court-ball. In a bed in the corner of the room her little boy is lying ill. He has a fever, and is asking for oranges. His mother has nothing to give him but river water, so he is crying. Swallow, Swallow, little Swallow, will you not take her the ruby out of my sword-hilt? My feet are fastened to this pedestal and I cannot move."

"I am waited for in Egypt," said the Swallow. "My friends are flying up and down the Nile."

"Swallow, Swallow, little Swallow," said the Prince, "will you not stay with me for one night, and be my messenger? The boy is so thirsty, and the mother so sad."

"I don't think I like boys," answered the Swallow. "Last summer, when I was staying on the river, there were two rude boys, the miller's sons, who were always throwing stones at me. They never hit me, of course; we swallows fly far too well for that, and besides, I come of a family famous for its swiftness; but still it was a mark of disrespect."

But the Happy Prince looked so sad that the little Swallow was sorry. "It is very cold here," he said; "but I will stay with you for one night and be your messenger."

"Thank you, little Swallow," said the Prince.

So the Swallow picked out the great ruby from the Prince's sword, and flew away with it in his beak over the roofs of the town.

He passed by the cathedral tower, where the white marble angels were sculptured. He passed by the palace and heard a beautiful girl say, "I hope my dress will be ready in time for the State-ball. I have ordered flowers to be embroidered on it; but the seamstresses are so lazy."

At last he came to the poor house and looked in. The boy was tossing feverishly on his bed, and the mother had fallen asleep, she was so tired. In he hopped, and laid the great ruby on the table beside the woman's thimble. Then he flew gently round the bed, fanning the boy's forehead with his wings. "How cool I feel," said the boy, "I must be getting better;" and he sank into a delicious slumber.

Then the Swallow flew back to the Happy Prince. "It is strange," he remarked, "but I feel quite warm now, although it is so cold."

"That is because you have done a good action," said the Prince. And the little Swallow began to think, and then he fell asleep. Thinking always made him sleepy.

When day broke he flew down to the river and had a bath. "What a remarkable phenomenon," said the Bird Professor as he was passing over the bridge. "A swallow in winter!" And he wrote a long letter about it to the local newspaper.

"To-night I go to Egypt," said the Swallow, and he was in high spirits. He visited all the public monuments, and sat a long time on top of the church steeple. Wherever he went the Sparrows chirruped, and said to each other, "What a distinguished stranger!" so he enjoyed himself very much.

When the moon rose he flew back to the Happy Prince. "Have you any commissions for Egypt?" he cried; "I am just starting."

"Swallow, Swallow, little Swallow," said the Prince, "will you not stay with me one night longer?"

"I am waited for in Egypt," answered the Swallow. "To-morrow my friends will fly up to the Second Cataract. The river-horse couches there among the bulrushes. At noon the lions come down to the water's edge to drink. They have eyes like green beryls, and their roar is louder than the roar of the cataract."

"Swallow, Swallow, little Swallow," said the Prince, "far away across the city I see a young man in a garret. He is leaning over a desk covered with papers. He is trying to finish a play, but he is too cold to write any more. There is no fire in the grate, and hunger has made him faint."

"I will wait with you one night longer," said the Swallow, who really had a good heart. "Shall I take him another ruby?"

"Alas!" said the Prince; "my eyes are all that I have left. But they are made of rare sapphires, brought out of India a thousand years ago. Pluck out one of them and take it to him. He will sell it to the jeweler, and buy food and firewood, and finish his play."

"Dear Prince," said the Swallow, "I cannot do that;" and he began to weep.

"Swallow, Swallow, little Swallow," said the Prince, "do as I command you."

So the Swallow plucked out the Prince's eye, and flew away to the student's garret. It was easy enough to get in, as there was a hole in the roof. Through this he darted, and came into the room. The young man had his head buried in his hands, so he did not hear the flutter of the bird's wings, and when he looked up he found the beautiful sapphire.

"Now I can finish my play," he cried, and he looked quite happy.

The next day the Swallow flew down to the harbor. He sat on the mast of a large vessel and watched the sailors hauling big chests out of the hold with ropes. "Heave a-hoy!" they shouted as each chest came up. "I am going to Egypt," cried the Swallow, but nobody minded, and when the moon rose he flew back to the Happy Prince.

"I am come to bid you good-by," he cried.

"Swallow, Swallow, little Swallow," said the Prince, "will you not stay with me one night longer?"

"It is winter," answered the Swallow, "and the chill snow will soon be here. In Egypt the sun is warm on the green palm-trees, and the crocodiles lie in the mud. My companions are building a nest. Dear Prince, I must leave you, but I will never forget you, and next spring I will bring you back two beautiful jewels in place of those you have given away. The ruby shall be redder than a red rose, and the sapphire shall be as blue as the great sea."

"In the square below," said the Happy Prince, "there stands a little match-girl. She has let her matches fall in the gutter, and they are all spoiled. Her father will beat her if she does not take home some money, and she is crying. She has no shoes or stockings, and her little head is bare. Pluck out my other eye, and give it to her, and her father will not beat her."

"I will stay with you one night longer," said the Swallow, "but I cannot pluck out your eye. You would be quite blind then."

"Swallow, Swallow, little Swallow," said the Prince, "do as I command you."

So he plucked out the Prince's other eye, and darted down with it. He swooped past the match-girl, and slipped the jewel into the palm of her hand. "What a lovely bit of glass!" cried the little girl; and she ran home, laughing.

Then the Swallow came back to the Prince. "You are blind now," he said, "so I will stay with you always."

"No, little Swallow," said the poor Prince, "you must go away to Egypt."

"I will stay with you always," said the Swallow, and he slept at the Prince's feet.

All the next day he sat on the Prince's shoulder, and told him stories of what he had seen in strange lands. He told him of the red ibises, who stand in long rows on the banks of the Nile, and catch gold-fish in their beaks; and of the Sphinx, who is as old as the world itself, and lives in the desert, and knows everything.

"Dear little Swallow," said the Prince, "you tell me of marvelous things, but fly over my city, little Swallow, and tell me what you see there."

So the Swallow flew over the great city, and saw the rich making merry in their beautiful houses, while the beggars were sitting at the gates. He flew into dark lanes, and saw the white faces of starving children looking out listlessly at the black streets. Under the archway of a bridge two little boys were lying in one another's arms to try and keep themselves warm. "How hungry we are!" they said. "You must not lie here," shouted the Watchman, and they wandered out into the rain.

Then he flew back and told the Prince what he had seen.

"I am covered with fine gold," said the Prince, "you must take it off, leaf by leaf, and give it to my poor."

Leaf after leaf of the fine gold the Swallow picked off, till the Happy Prince looked quite dull and gray. Leaf after leaf of the fine gold he took to the poor. "We have bread now!" they cried. And the children's faces grew rosier, and they laughed and played games in the street.

Then the snow came, and after the snow came the frost. The streets looked as if they were made of silver, they were so bright and glistening; long icicles like crystal daggers hung down from the eaves of the houses.

The poor little Swallow grew colder and colder, but he would not leave the Prince; he loved him too well. He picked up crumbs outside the baker's door, and tried to keep himself warm by flapping his wings.

But at last he knew that he was going to die. He had just strength to fly up to the Prince's shoulder once more. "Good-by, dear Prince!" he murmured. "Will you let me kiss your hand?"

"I am glad that you are going to Egypt at last, little Swallow," said the Prince, "you have stayed too long here; but kiss me on the lips, for I love you."

"It is not to Egypt that I am going," said the Swallow. "I am going to Death. Death is the brother of Sleep, is he not?"

And he kissed the happy Prince on the lips, and fell down dead at his feet.

At that moment a curious crack sounded inside the statue, as if something had broken. The fact is that the leaden heart had snapped in two. It certainly was a hard frost.

Early the next morning the Mayor was walking in the square below in company with the Town Councilors. As they passed the column he looked up at the statue. "Dear me! how shabby the Happy Prince looks!" he said.

"How shabby indeed!" cried the Town Councilors, who always agreed with the Mayor, and they went up to look at it.

"The ruby has fallen out of his sword, his eyes are gone," said the Mayor; "in fact, he is little better than a beggar!"

So they pulled down the statue of the Happy Prince and sent it to be melted in a furnace.

"What a strange thing!" said the overseer of the workmen at the foundry. "This broken lead heart will not melt in the furnace. We must throw it away." So they threw it on a dust-heap where the dead Swallow was also lying.

"Bring me the two precious things in the city," said God to one of His Angels; and the Angel took Him the leaden heart and the dead bird.

"You have chosen rightly," said God; "in my garden of Paradise this little bird shall sing for evermore, and in my city of gold the Happy Prince shall praise me."

—OSCAR WILDE

THE DWARF ROOTS' STORY OF THE PUMPKIN SEED

Did you ever hear the story of the Pumpkin Seed that made a feast of his insides, and found his outsides changed most surprisingly, and went down a pig's throat and was happy? Ever since it happened the Dwarf Roots, who live below the ground, tell it to the pumpkin seeds. They say they heard it from the wind one day when the farmer's spade laid the ground open and let the wind in. And the wind says he heard the farm children's grandmother tell it. And she says she heard it from her grandmother. So you see it is an old story, and time you heard it. Then

>Throw the nuts in
>
>And let us straight begin.

Before the Dwarf Roots tell the story they stroke their beards that have grown fast into the ground, like hairy threads, and cry out, "Once upon a, twice upon a, thrice upon a time;" and all the little pumpkin seeds lying low in the ground know a story is coming and swell with joy. After that the Dwarf Roots tell the story as 'twas told to me. So

>Throw the nuts in
>
>And turn the first about.
>
>And let's not stop again
>
>Until the tale is out.

Here's the tale.

Early in the spring, when things with legs all walk abroad and garden folks are born, a little Pumpkin Seed stuck his head above ground. He arrived with his cap on, as pumpkin seeds do, but as soon as possible he shook it off, and looked about him to find out what to do next. And who should he see come trotting down the garden path toward him but a little sniffing, squealing pig, poking his snout into everything and gobbling it up!

Now, how he came to know it the little Pumpkin Seed never could tell, but all of a sudden he sang out:

>"I'm for your betters,
>
>Not you, piggy wig,
>
>When juicy I've grown
>
>And round and big;
>
>Then I'll change into something
>
>Which winks and blinks
>
>And with boys and girls
>
>Plays high jinks;

But when I'm out,

Snip, snap, snout,

You may have me,

It's your turn to shout."

The little pig was so astonished that he stood straight up on his hind legs and curled his tail in a tight knot, for all the world as if he were a performing pig in a circus. When he was firm on his legs again, he was just going to open his mouth, when he saw the farmer coming down the path, so he ran squealing from the garden. Some Dwarf Roots who tell the story say he was going to gobble up the little Pumpkin, and others say he was going to answer in pig's rhyme:

"When it's time to shout,

With my sniffy snout

I'll smell you out."

However that may be, the next time he came trotting that way he poked his snout into a wire netting the farmer had put around the kitchen garden to keep him out, so that was the last the little Pumpkin Seed saw of him for many a long day.

But the Pumpkin Seed knew now what he should do. He stood up straight in the sunlight and soft rain, and grew and grew and covered himself with blossoms, and then let them all drop off except one. And out of that he made a little pumpy pumpkin, and by harvest time he had that so fat and round and yellow and juicy that the Dwarf Roots' mouths water when they tell of it.

The farmer gathered the Pumpkin in a great basket, and his wife scooped out the splendid insides of it and made of them deep rich pies for the Thanksgiving feast that the farmer's family eat together in thankfulness to God for health and plenty. Everyone comes to the feast: grandfather and grandmother and uncles and aunts and all the children, first cousins and second cousins and third cousins and fourth cousins and fifth cousins, down to the littlest babies that can do nothing, when they're not feeding and sleeping, but gurgle and crow at their fingers and toes. To be sure, when the grown-ups bite into the deep rich pumpkin pie they can do nothing either but gurgle and smack their lips.

So it was that the inside of the Pumpkin did its part and made a feast and came to glory.

But what of the outside? You shall hear. It happened that very night.

The outside fell into the hands of a boy who could work surprising changes in things. He worked one in the outside of the Pumpkin. Some Dwarf Roots say he turned it into a Jack-o'-lantern, and some say into a goblin. Anyway, there it was that night, stuck in the farmer's hitching-post and changed most surprisingly. It had a head that glowed like fire in the darkness, and big round eyes that winked and blinked every time the wind blew, and a mouth that grinned from ear to ear when the big boys and girls made the little ones run past it. The little ones would steal up softly, and just when they were near the fiery head the big ones would cry out, "Look out, little uns, the goblin'll get cher"; and the little ones would dash past, laughing and shrieking.

So it was that the outside of the Pumpkin did its part and played high jinks with the children. Great fun it was; and it kept up until the farmer called out, "Time for bed, boys and girls."

Just as he said this the wind put the fire out of the Pumpkin's head and blew him off the hitching post. And the next thing he knew he was going down a pig's throat, the very piggy wig he met so long ago.

Snip, snap, snout,

This tale's out:

The pig has him now,

And it's his turn to shout.

—ANGELA M. KEYES

A HORSE'S STORY

Here is a story told by Black Beauty, as pretty a little horse as ever wore a white star on his forehead.

One day late in the autumn my master had a long journey to go on business. I was put to the dog-cart, and John, the coachman, drove. There had been a great deal of rain, and now the wind was very high and blew the dry leaves across the road in a shower. We went along merrily till we came to the toll-bar and the low wooden bridge. The river banks were rather high, and the bridge, instead of rising, went across just level, so that in the middle, if the river was full, the water would be nearly up to the woodwork and planks. But as there were good, substantial rails on each side, people did not mind it.

The man at the gate said the river was rising fast, and he feared it would be a bad night. Many of the meadows were under water, and in one low part of the road the water was halfway up to my knees. The bottom was good, however, and master drove gently, so it was no matter.

When we got to the town I had, of course, a good feed, but as the master's business engaged him a long time, we did not start for home till rather late in the afternoon. The wind was then much higher, and I heard the master say to John we had never been out in such a storm. And so I thought, as we went along the skirts of a wood, where the great branches were swaying about like twigs, and the rushing sound was terrible.

"I wish we were well out of this wood," said my master.

"Yes, sir," said John, "it would be rather awkward if one of these branches came down on us."

The words were scarcely out of his mouth when there was a groan, and a crack, and a splitting sound. And crashing down amongst the older trees came an oak, torn up by the roots. It fell across the road just before us. I will never say I was not frightened, for I was. I stopped still, and I believe I trembled. Of course I did not turn round or run away; I was not brought up to that. John jumped out and in a moment was at my head.

"That came very near," said my master. "What's to be done now?"

"Well, sir, we can't drive over that tree, nor yet get round it. There's nothing for us but to go back to the four cross-ways, and that will be a good six miles before we get round to the wooden bridge again. It will make us late, but the horse is fresh."

So back we went and round by the cross roads. By the time we got to the bridge it was very nearly dark. We could just see that the water was over the middle of it. As this sometimes happened when there were floods, master did not stop. We were going along at a good pace, but the moment my feet touched the first part of the bridge, I felt sure there was something wrong. I dared not go forward, and I made a dead stop. "Go on, Beauty," said my master, and he gave me a touch with the whip, but I dared not stir. He gave me a sharp cut. I jumped, but I dared not go forward.

"There's something wrong, sir," said John, and he sprang out of the dog-cart, and came to my head and looked all about. He tried to lead me forward. "Come on, Beauty; what's the matter?" Of course, I could not tell him, but I knew very well that the bridge was not safe.

Just then the man at the toll-gate on the other side ran out of the house, tossing a torch about violently.

"Hoy, hoy, hoy! halloo! stop!" he cried.

"What's the matter?" shouted my master.

"The bridge is broken in the middle, and part of it is carried away; if you come on you'll be into the river."

"Thank God!" said my master. "You Beauty!" said John, and took the bridle and gently turned me round to the right-hand road by the river side. The sun had set some time. The wind seemed to have lulled off after that furious blast which tore up the tree. It grew darker and darker, stiller and stiller. I trotted quietly along, the wheels hardly making a sound on the soft road. For a good while neither master nor John spoke, and then master began in a serious voice. I could not understand much of what they said, but I found they thought that if I had gone on as the master wanted me, horse, chaise, master, and man would have fallen into the river. Master said, God had given men reason, by which they could find out things for themselves; but he had given animals instinct, which did not depend on reason, and which was much more prompt and perfect in its way, and by which they had often saved the lives of men.

At last we came to the park gates, and found the gardener looking out for us. He said that mistress had been much alarmed ever since dark, fearing some accident had happened, and that she had sent James off on Justice, the roan cob, towards the wooden bridge to make inquiry after us.

We saw a light at the hall door and at the upper windows, and as we came up, mistress ran out, saying to master, "Are you really safe, my dear? Oh! I have been so anxious, fancying all sorts of things. Have you had no accident?"

"No, but if your Black Beauty had not been wiser than we were, we should all have been carried down the river at the wooden bridge." I heard no more, as they went into the house, and John took me to the stable. Oh, what a good supper he gave me that night, a good bran mash and some crushed beans with my oats, and such a thick bed of straw! and I was glad of it, for I was tired.

—ANNA SEWELL

A BEWITCHED DONKEY

There was once a little donkey who lived with a little old woman and her tabby cat and her rooster and his hens and their chicks in a little cottage out in the country. Every morning, after cropping the dewy grass, the little donkey used to poke his head in at the cottage window, as much as to say, "It's time we were off," and the little old woman used to say, "I'll be with you in two shakes of Tabby's tail." Presently out she would bring two baskets of fresh-laid eggs from the hens and hang them across the donkey's back, and off to market they'd go. Tabby would stop washing her face to wave her paw at them, and the little old woman would wave her hand back, and the little donkey would turn and wave his head. They were as happy and loving as any people that ever lived together, and the donkey was the man of the family.

But one morning something got into the donkey. He seemed to be bewitched. You shall hear.

When he had cropped the dewy grass as usual, he poked his head in at the cottage window, as much as to say, "It's time we were off," and the little old woman said, "I'll be with you in two shakes of Tabby's tail." But the minute she came to the door with the two baskets of fresh-laid eggs from the hens, up went the little donkey's heels, and away he ran with such a kick and a run and a run and a kick that the little old woman couldn't keep up with him were she never so quick. All at once she was so surprised at him that she stood stock still. Immediately stock still stood the little donkey and laughed at her till his fat little sides shook, "Hee haw, hee haw, hee haw." This was too much for the little old woman. "Can it be that my own little donkey is laughing at his little old woman?" she said. And one basket of eggs dropped smash on the ground and she began to cry.

At this out came Tabby, and up came running all the hens and their little chicks and the lordly rooster, and they all rubbed against the little old woman's skirts, and Tabby miowed, "Our little old woman, do not cry," and the hens cackled it, and the little chicks peeped it, and the rooster crowed it. And then they all said it together, each in his own way.

"But the man of the family has run away from us and he laughs at it," said the little old woman; "whatever shall we do!"

"Let us give him another chance," said the big white hen with the kind face. "Begin all over again and see what happens."

So the rooster led the way back to the yard, and the hens followed him and the little chicks followed them. At the same time Tabby led the way back to the cottage and the little old woman followed her. When the little old woman was inside she began packing the one basket of eggs into the two baskets. Well, sure enough, the little donkey did his part, too. He ran back and began cropping the dewy grass, and then he poked his head in at the cottage window as much as to say, "It's time we were off," and the little old woman in high glee called out, "I'll be with you in two shakes of Tabby's tail."

But the minute she came to the door with the two baskets of fresh-laid eggs from the hens, up went the little donkey's heels, and away he ran with such a kick and a run and a run and a kick that the little old woman couldn't keep up with him were she never so quick. And as before, all at once she was so surprised at him that she stood stock still. Immediately stock still stood the little donkey and laughed at her till his fat little sides shook, "Hee haw, hee haw, hee haw." And, as before, this was too much for the little old woman. "Can it be that my own little donkey is laughing at his little old woman?" she said. And one basket of eggs dropped smash on the ground and she began to cry.

At this out came Tabby, and up came running all the hens and their little chicks and the lordly rooster, and they all rubbed against the little old woman's skirts, and Tabby miowed, "Our little old woman, do not cry," and the hens cackled it, and the little chicks peeped it, and the rooster crowed it. And then they all said it together, each in his own way.

So it was of no use.

But at last the little old woman thought of a plan, such an easy thing, too, and sure to be what a little old woman would think of sooner or later to keep the man of the family. Instead of staying in the cottage, when they went back to try it over a third time, she went out by a back door and crept around the side of the house. When the donkey poked his head in at the window she ran out, caught him by the heels, shoved him in, jumped in after him, and held him. The lordly rooster and the hen and the little chicks were watching, and they ran in and shut both doors fast. And then they all waited and listened, and presently the donkey began to explain himself.

The moonlight the night before was so strong, he said, that it woke him up. As he opened his eyes he heard little voices, as sweet as silver bells, singing,

> "O lovely moon, queen of the night,
>
> Beautiful moon, glorious and bright,
>
> Hail, all hail!"

He looked out of his shed into the moonlight, and there on the green he saw the most exquisite fairies, with wings shining with all the colors of the rainbow, hand in hand with big-eyed tiny elves with bumpy heads and little legs. They were all dancing in a ring and looking up at the moon. And the moon was gazing down at them.

Now he knew very well that the fairy folk do not like to be spied on; he had often heard the little old woman tell it to her gossip, Tabby, the cat. And she had warned him to stay in his stall and not go prying on the night folk. And he said he was truly sorry now that he did it, but at the time he thought it would be fun. So he stole up around a stack of hay near where they were dancing in honor of the moon, and all at once he gave such a bray that the fairies fell to the ground in little swoons, and the elves jumped so high into the air that for a whole second he lost sight of them.

But the moonlight showed *them* where he was. Quick as a wink they whipped little horns out of their belts and blew together three times. Up came hobbling from the shadows an old witch. She saw the donkey at once, and pointing her long finger at his heels cried,

> "Kick him, heels,
>
> Until he feels
>
> Ashamed to spy
>
> At fairy reels,
>
> He-he-he!
>
> He must kick
>
> And run away,
>
> And fill the air
>
> With donkey bray,
>
> Until he eats
>
> A wisp of hay
>
> Given by bat
>
> Or by cat."

Well, Tabby was off to a stable before one shake of her own tail, and presently back she came with the wisp of hay. The little old woman gave it to the little donkey and held her breath to see what would happen, and so did Tabby and the lordly rooster and the hens and the little chicks. No sooner had the donkey swallowed it than he left off kicking and trying to run away!

So now, of course, everything came right. The lordly rooster led his wives and children back to the henyard, and the little old woman and the little donkey set off to market with the eggs that had not been smashed. Tabby stopped washing her face to wave her paw at them, and the little old woman waved her hand back, and the little donkey turned and waved his head.

And ever after they were as loving and happy as any people that ever lived together, and the donkey was the man of the family.

—Angela M. Keyes

THE STRAW, THE COAL, AND THE BEAN

(Tell with stick-figure blackboard illustrations.)

In a village there lived an old woman who one day gathered some beans from her garden to cook. She had a good fire on the hearth, but, to make it burn more quickly, she threw on a handful of straw. As she threw the beans into the pot to boil, one of them fell on the floor unseen by the old woman, not far from a wisp of straw. Suddenly a glowing coal bounced out of the fire, and fell close to them. They both started away, and exclaimed, "Dear friend, don't come near me till you are cooler. Whatever brings you out here?"

"Oh," replied the coal, "the heat luckily made me so strong that I was able to bounce from the fire. Had I not done so, my death would have been certain, and I should have been burnt to ashes by this time."

"I, too, have escaped with a whole skin," said the bean; "for had the old woman put me into the pot with my comrades, I should have been boiled to broth."

"I might have shared the same fate," said the straw, "for all my brothers were pushed into fire and smoke by the old woman. She seized sixty of us at once, and brought us in here to take away our lives, but luckily I slipped through her fingers."

"Well, now what shall we do with ourselves?" said the coal.

"I think," answered the bean, "as we have been so fortunate as to escape death together, we may as well be companions, and travel away together to some more friendly country."

This pleased the two others; so they started on their journey together. After traveling a little distance, they came to a stream, over which there was no bridge of any sort.

Then the straw thought of a plan, and said, "I will lay myself across the stream, so that you may step over me, as if I were a bridge."

So the straw stretched himself from one shore to the other, and the coal, who was rather hot-headed, tripped out quite boldly on the newly built bridge. But when he reached the middle of the stream, and heard the water rushing under him, he was so frightened that he stood still, and dared not move a step farther. The straw began to burn, broke in two, and fell into the brook. The coal slid after him, hissed as he reached the water, and gave up the ghost.

The bean, who had cautiously remained behind on the shore, could not keep in when she saw what had happened, and laughed so heartily that she burst her sides. It would have been all over with her, too; but, as good luck would have it, a tailor, out on his travels, came to rest by the brook, and noticed the bean. He was a kind-hearted man, so he took a needle and thread out of his pocket, and, taking up the bean, sewed her together. She thanked him prettily, but unfortunately he had only black thread to sew with, and so since that time all beans have a black seam down their sides.

—FOLK TALE

MOTHER HOLLE

There was once a widow who had two daughters. One of them was pretty and industrious, but the other was ugly and idle. Now the mother was much fonder of the ugly and idle one, because this was her own daughter. She made the other do all the work, and be the Cinderella of the house. Every day the poor girl had to sit by a well, in the highway, and spin and spin till her fingers bled.

One day as she worked the shuttle got marked with her blood, so she dipped it into the well, to wash the mark off. But it dropped out of her hand and fell to the bottom. She began to weep, and ran to her mother and told her of the mishap. But the mother scolded her sharply, and was so cruel as to say, "As you have let the shuttle fall in, you must fetch it out again."

The girl went back to the well, and did not know what to do. In the sorrow of her heart she jumped into the well, and lost her senses from fright.

When she awoke and came to herself again, she was in a beautiful meadow where the sun was shining and many thousands of flowers were growing. Along this meadow she went, and came to a baker's oven full of bread, and the bread cried out,

"Oh, take me out!

Take me out!

Or I shall burn;

I have baked a long time!"

So she went up to it, and took out all the loaves, one after another, with the bread-shovel. After that she went on till she came to a tree covered with apples, which called out to her,

"Oh, shake me!

Shake me!

We apples are all ripe!"

So she shook the tree till the apples fell like rain, and went on shaking till they were all down, and when she had gathered them into a heap, she went on her way.

At last she came to a little house out of which peeped an old woman. The old woman had such large teeth that the girl was frightened, and was about to run away.

But the old woman said, "What are you afraid of, dear child? Stay with me; if you will do all the work in the house properly, you shall be the better for it. Only you must take care to make my bed well, and to shake it thoroughly till the feathers fly—for then there is snow on the earth. I am Mother Holle."

The old woman spoke so kindly to her, the girl took courage and agreed to enter her service. She did everything so well that she pleased her mistress, and always shook her bed so vigorously that the feathers flew about like snowflakes. She had a pleasant life with the old woman, never an angry word, and boiled or roast meat every day.

But after she had stayed some time with Mother Holle, she became sad. At first she did not know what was the matter with her, but at last she felt it was homesickness. Although she was many thousand times better off here than at home, still she had a longing to be there. So one day she said to the old woman, "I wish I were home, no matter how well off I am down here, I cannot stay any longer; I must go up again to my own people." Mother Holle said, "I am glad that you long for your home, and as you have served me so truly, I myself will take you up again." She took her by the hand, and led her to a large door. The door opened, and just as the maiden was standing beneath the door-way, a heavy shower of golden rain fell, and all the gold remained on her, so that she was covered with it.

"You shall have that because you are so industrious," said Mother Holle; and at the same time she gave her back the shuttle which the girl had let fall into the well. Then the door closed, and the maiden found herself up above the earth, not far from her mother's house.

As she went into the yard, the cock standing by the well-side cried,

> "Cock-a-doodle-doo!
>
> Your golden girl's come back to you!"

So she went in to her mother. And because she arrived covered with gold, her mother and sister were glad to have her back.

The girl told all that had happened to her. As soon as the mother heard how she had come by so much gold, she was very anxious that the same good luck should come to the ugly and lazy daughter. So she made *her* seat herself by the well and spin. But the idle girl did not work. To stain the spindle with blood, she stuck her hand into a thorn bush and pricked her finger. Then she threw the shuttle into the well, and jumped in after it.

She came, like the other, to the beautiful meadow and walked along the very same path. When she came to the oven, the bread again cried,

> "Oh, take me out!
>
> Take me out!
>
> Or I shall burn;
>
> I have baked a long time!"

But the lazy thing answered, "As if I had any wish to make myself dirty?" and on she went. Soon she came to the apple-tree, which cried,

> "Oh, shake me!
>
> Shake me!
>
> We apples are all ripe!"

But she answered, "I like that! One of you might fall on my head," and so went on.

When she came to Mother Holle's house, she was not afraid, for she had already heard of her big teeth, and she hired herself to her immediately.

The first day she forced herself to work diligently, and obeyed Mother Holle when she told her to do anything, for she was thinking of all the gold she would give her. But on the second day she began to be lazy, and on the third day still more so, and then she would not get up in the morning at all.

Neither did she make Mother Holle's bed as she ought, and did not shake it so as to make the feathers fly up. Mother Holle was soon tired of this, and gave her notice to leave. The lazy girl was willing enough to go, and thought that now the golden rain would come. Mother Holle led her, too, to the great door; but while she was standing beneath it, instead of the gold a big kettle of black pitch was emptied over her. "That is the reward of your service," said Mother Holle, and shut the door.

So the lazy girl went home; but she was quite covered with pitch, and the cock by the well-side, as soon as he saw her, cried out,

"Cock-a-doodle-doo!

Your pitchy girl's come back to you!"

And the pitch stuck fast to her, and could not be got off as long as she lived.

—FOLK TALE

TOM THUMB

(Arranged as a continued story)

HOW HE CAME TO HIS MOTHER AND FATHER

Long, long ago, when good King Arthur ruled in Britain, there lived a magician named Merlin. He could change himself into anything he chose, and one day when he had changed himself into a beggar he stopped at a plowman's cottage to ask for food.

"Come in, poor fellow," cried the plowman, "there's always a bite for another." And the plowman's wife set on the table a bowl of milk and a platter heaped with sweet brown bread. Merlin was greatly pleased with the good people's kindness to him.

Now, by and by he noticed that although everything in the cottage was neat and comfortable, something was troubling these kind people. So he asked them what it was.

"Ah," cried the poor woman, with tears in her eyes, "we have no little son. If I only had a little son, I should be the happiest woman in the world, even if he were no bigger than my husband's thumb."

Well, Merlin said nothing, and when he had rested he went on his way.

But he did not forget the kind people's sorrow. As soon as he could, he paid a visit to the queen of the fairies, and told her about it and begged her to grant the woman's wish. Sure enough, after a time the plowman's wife had a little son, and lo and behold! he was not a bit bigger than her husband's thumb. While his mother was admiring him, the queen of the fairies came in at the window. She kissed the child and called him Tom Thumb. She sent for some of the fairies to dress him, and she herself told what he should wear.

So the fairies came and dressed the little man according to the queen's directions:

"An oak leaf hat he had for a crown;

His shirt of web by spiders spun;

With jacket wove of thistle down;

His trousers were of feathers done.

His stockings, of apple-rind, they tie

With eyelash from his mother's eye;

His shoes were made of mouse's skin,

Tann'd with the downy hair within."

So it was that Tom Thumb, the fairy mannikin, came into the world; and, wonderful to tell, he never grew any bigger than his father's thumb.

TOM THUMB

How He Grows up Full of Tricks

But as he got older he grew to be full of tricks.

He used to play cherry-stones with the boys. When he had lost all his own stones, he would creep slyly into his playmates' bags, quickly fill his pockets with their stones, creep out unseen, and join again in the game.

One day as he did this the boy who owned the bag caught him at it. "Ah, ha! my little Tommy," he cried, "at last I have caught you stealing my cherry-stones. I'll teach you to stop that." And he quickly drew the string, shutting Tom into the bag, and gave the bag such a shake that the poor little fellow's legs and thighs and body were sadly bruised. Tom roared with pain and promised never to do that again.

So he was cured of that trick.

TOM THUMB

How He Has a Narrow Escape from a Batter Pudding

A short time afterwards Tom's mother was making a batter pudding for supper, and inquisitive little Tom must of course see how it was made. So he climbed up to the edge of the bowl; but unfortunately his foot slipped and in he plumped, head and ears, into the batter. His mother, poor woman, never caught sight nor light of him, so she stirred him into the batter and put it into the pot to boil.

Now, the batter had filled Tom's mouth and kept him from crying out to his mother. But when he felt the water getting hot, he kicked and struggled so much in the pot that his mother thought the pudding must be bewitched. She pulled it out of the pot and threw it outdoors. A poor tinker crying, "Pots to mend, kettles to mend," was passing in the nick of time, so, thinking it would make him a good dinner, he stuffed it into his pack and walked off with it. By this time Tom's mouth was clear of the batter, so he yelled lustily to be let out. The terrified tinker flung down his pack and ran away. The pudding broke to pieces, and Tom crept out, covered with batter, but glad to be alive and to make his way home as fast as he could.

When Tom's mother saw the state of her darling she was ready to weep. She put him into a teacup of warm water and washed off the mess. Then, forgetting the loss of her pudding, she kissed him and tucked him into bed.

TOM THUMB

How He Gets into the Red Cow's Stomach

Well, soon after the batter pudding mischief, Tom's mother went to milk her cow in the meadow, and she took Tom along with her. As the wind was strong she was afraid he might be blown away, so she took out of her pocket a piece of fine thread and tied him to a thistle. Then she set about milking the cow.

It wasn't long before the cow caught sight of Tom's oak leaf hat, and thrusting out her tongue she took in poor Tom and the thistle at a mouthful. Tom was terrified. But while the cow was chewing the thistle he had time to collect his wits, although he was afraid every minute her monstrous teeth would crush him in pieces. So he roared out as loudly as he could, "Mother, mother!"

"Where are you, Tommy, my darling? where are you?" cried his mother, dropping her milking.

"Here, mother," he shouted, "here, in the red cow's mouth."

At this his poor mother began to cry and wring her hands, looking helplessly at the cow. But what was her joy! The cow, surprised at the odd noise in her throat, opened her mouth and let Tom drop out. Quick as a flash his mother caught him up before he could fall to the ground, and she ran home with him.

TOM THUMB

HOW HE COMES TO BELONG TO THE KING

One day when Tom went into the fields to drive the cattle with a whip of barley straw his father had given him, he slipped and rolled into one of the furrows. A raven flying overhead picked him up and flew with him to the top of a giant's castle near the sea, and there left him.

Tom did not know what to do. But this was not the worst of it. He heard a heavy tread, tramp! tramp! and out strode Grumbo, the giant who owned the castle. He saw Tom, picked him up and gulped him down in a twinkling, as if he were a pill. But in a minute he was sorry. For Tom began to kick and jump about so that the giant could not stand him in his stomach, but rushed to the castle wall and vomited him into the sea.

Well, the instant Tom struck the water a great fish swallowed him. Soon a fisherman caught this very fish, took it to market, and there sold it for King Arthur's own table. And when the king's cook cut the fish open, out stepped Tom, alive and well, and stood on his head for joy to find himself safe and free again. The astonished cook ran with him to the king, and Tom so delighted the king and queen and all the knights of the Round Table with his tricks that the king called him his dwarf, to make fun for him and the court.

In time the king grew so fond of Tom that he took him everywhere with him, and even let him creep into his pocket for shelter if it should rain when they were out together.

So now Tom Thumb was King Arthur's dwarf and lived at court.

TOM THUMB

HOW HE CARRIES MONEY TO HIS PARENTS

One day King Arthur asked Tom about his parents, whether they were as small as Tom, and whether they were rich or poor. Tom told the king his father and mother were as tall as any of the people at court but they were poor. At this the king took Tom into the treasury and told him to take home to his parents as much money as he could carry.

Tom capered for joy. He ran off to get a purse, and into this he stuffed a silver threepenny piece. He had some trouble hoisting the bag of money on his back, but at last he succeeded, and set out on his journey.

It was a short distance, but tiny Tom had to rest more than a hundred times by the way, so that it took him two days and two nights to reach his father's house. His mother ran out to meet him, and carried him into the house more dead than alive.

She and the father were overjoyed to see him, the more so as he had brought such a great sum of money; but they were grieved that he was so worn out. His mother placed him tenderly in a walnut shell, and feasted him three whole days on a hazel nut. To her sorrow this made him sick, for he should not have eaten a whole nut in less than a month.

In time, Tom was able to run about and to think of returning to court. But as there had been a heavy fall of rain his mother said the roads were too wet for him to walk. So when the wind was blowing in the direction of the king's castle she made a little umbrella of paper, tied Tom to it, gave him a puff into the air with her mouth, and away he went back to King Arthur.

TOM THUMB

How He Becomes Ill and Who Nurses Him

Well, Tom was never tired making fun for the king and queen and all the court. The courtiers laughed till their sides ached at his antics, and the king said to the queen, "Did you ever see the like?" And she said, "No, never!"

But he did so much, he at last made himself ill. The whole court was filled with sorrow, for everyone feared the little fellow would die. The king came constantly to his bedside to ask how he was, and brought his cleverest physicians to cure him. But they could not.

In the midst of their anxiety the queen of the fairies ordered her chariot drawn by winged butterflies, and set out for the palace. She lifted Tom tenderly out of his bed and carried him with her to fairyland. Here she herself nursed him back to health and let him play with the fairies until he was as strong and merry as ever.

Then she ordered a breeze to rise. And on this she placed Tom and sent him back to the king.

TOM THUMB

HOW TOM ESCAPES HANGING

Now, just as Tom came flying back to King Arthur's court, the cook happened to be passing with the king's great bowl of frumenty, a dish the king was very fond of. Unfortunately the little fellow fell plump into the middle of it, splashing the hot frumenty in the cook's face. The cook, in a rage at Tom for frightening and scalding him, ran to tell the king that Tom had jumped into his Majesty's favorite dish out of idle mischief.

The king's anger was terrible. He ordered Tom to be seized and tried. No one dared plead for him, so the king commanded that his head be cut off. A crowd followed the headsman to see it done. The headsman lifted his ax. Poor little Tom fell a-trembling and looked about for some means of escape. In the crowd he saw a miller with his mouth open, like the booby he was. At a bound Tom leaped into the miller's mouth. He sprang in so nimbly that no one, not even the miller himself, saw where he went. So, as the headsman could not find Tom to take off Tom's head, he, like a sensible man, shouldered his ax and went home; and the miller went back to his mill.

When Tom heard the miller at work in the mill, he knew he was far away from the court and entirely safe, so he immediately set about getting out. He began to roll and tumble about in such an alarming way that the miller took to bed and sent for a doctor. When the doctor arrived, Tom began to dance and sing, and the doctor, as much frightened as the miller, sent in hot haste for five more doctors and twenty learned men.

While the six doctors and the twenty learned men were putting their wise heads together, the miller happened to yawn. Seizing the chance, Tom took another jump, but out of the miller's mouth this time, and alighted safe on his feet in the middle of a table near the bed. Well, when the miller saw the little bit of a creature that had tormented him, it was his turn to fall into a rage at Tom. He laid hands on him, opened the window, and threw him into the river.

And a second time Tom was swallowed by a fish! A large salmon swimming along snapped him up. A fisherman caught the salmon and sold it in the market for a great lord's table. But when the lord saw it he thought it such a fine fish that he made a present of it to King Arthur. So when the cook cut open the fish he found poor Tom and ran to the king with him to make sure that he should not escape again. But the king was busy and ordered Tom to be kept locked up until he should send for him.

The cook was determined that Tom should not get away, so he put him into a mouse trap closely wired. When Tom had spent a week in the trap peeping through the wires, the king sent for him. But to the cook's disappointment and Tom's great delight, his anger had gone. He forgave Tom for falling into the frumenty, and made him again his dwarf, to make fun for him and the court.

TOM THUMB

HOW HE IS KNIGHTED BY THE KING

To reward Tom for his services to the court, the king made him a knight. He told Tom to kneel down. Then he struck him with his sword and said, "With this sword I dub thee knight. Arise, Sir Thomas Thumb."

As Tom's clothes had suffered in the batter pudding, the frumenty, and the insides of the giant, the miller, and the fishes, the king ordered that the new knight should be given a handsome suit of clothes and a horse and sword. How proud Tom was and how splendid he looked! You shall hear about his dress and his horse and sword:

> Of butterfly's wings his shirt was made,
>
> His boots of chicken's hide;
>
> And by a nimble fairy blade,
>
> Well learned in the tailoring trade,
>
> His clothing was supplied.—
>
> A needle dangled by his side;
>
> A dapper mouse he used to ride,
>
> Thus strutted Tom in lordly pride.

It was great fun to see Tom mounted on the mouse, as he rode out a-hunting with the king and the other knights. They were all ready to die with laughter as they looked at him and his prancing charger.

But they were glad to call him a brother knight, he was so brave.

One day as they were riding past a farmhouse a large cat lurking about a door made a spring at Tom and the mouse, seized them, and ran up a tree with them. Here she began to devour the mouse. Tom boldly drew his sword and stuck it into the cat so fiercely that she was at last forced to drop them. As they fell, one of the knights held out his hat and caught them. He carried Tom home and laid him on a bed of down in a little ivory cabinet until he should get over the attack.

Tom was soon himself again, and dearer than ever to the king and court.

TOM THUMB

How He Goes Away and Comes Back Again

Soon after, the queen of the fairies came to pay Tom a visit, and when she left she took Tom back with her to fairyland. There he stayed several years.

While he was gone King Arthur and the queen and all the knights who knew Tom died, so when he came back he found a new king reigning, King Thunstone. All the courtiers flocked about the mannikin, and asked him who he was, and whence he came, and where he lived. Tom answered,

> "My name is Tom Thumb,
>
> From the fairies I've come.
>
> When King Arthur shone,
>
> This court was my home.
>
> In me he delighted,
>
> By him I was knighted;
>
> Have you never heard of Sir Thomas Thumb?"

The king was so charmed with this speech that he at once made Tom court dwarf. He ordered his builders to build Tom a gold palace a span high, with a door an inch wide, and he ordered his coachmen to give Tom a coach drawn by six small mice. And so that he might sit upon the king's table close to his elbow, he ordered his cabinet makers to make Tom a little ivory chair.

So there was Tom back at court again and king's favorite.

TOM THUMB

What Became of Him at Last

But Tom did not live much longer. A large spider one day attacked him. Tom drew his sword and fought well, but at last the spider's poisonous breath overcame him.

> "He fell dead on the ground where he stood,
>
> And the spider suck'd up every drop of his blood."

Well, of course he had to die some time.

King Thunstone and his whole court were so sorry that they went into mourning for him, and over his grave they raised a white marble monument. And the king's engraver wrote this on it:

"Here lyes Tom Thumb, King Arthur's knight,

Who died by a cruel spider's bite.

He was well known in Arthur's court,

Where he afforded gallant sport;

He rode at tilt and tournament,

And on a mouse a-hunting went.

Alive he filled the court with mirth;

His death to sorrow soon gave birth.

Wipe, wipe your eyes, and shake your head

And cry,—'Alas! Tom Thumb is dead!'"

—ENGLISH FOLK TALE

THE TWO BROTHERS

Once upon a time there were two brothers. Each had ten loaves of bread and nothing else. So they said, "Let us go and seek our fortune." And they went.

When they had gone a little way they were hungry. One brother said to the other, "Come, let us eat thy bread first, then we shall eat mine." So they did and went on their way. When they had gone farther they were hungry again. The first brother said again to the other, "Come, let us eat thy bread, then we shall eat mine." They did and went on their way. And when they had gone farther they finished the ten loaves. Then the first brother, who had yet kept *his* loaves, said to the other, "Now thou mayst go thy way, and I shall go mine. Thou hast no loaves left, and I will not let thee eat my bread." And the heartless fellow turned his back and left his brother to go on alone without a morsel of food.

Well, the brother went on and on and on, more and more feebly, for want of food, till he came to a mill in a dark forest. He said to the miller, "I can go no farther; pray let me stay here to-night."

Now the miller was a truer brother to him than his own had been, and he answered, "Brother, I would not turn thee away if it were safe. But wild beasts come into this wood at night, perhaps into this very mill. I myself do not wait to see."

"I feel no fear," said the poor boy; "the beasts will not harm me." So while the miller went off home he crept into the hopper of the mill.

At midnight from some place or other a big bear, a wolf, and a jackal came into the mill, and went leaping and bounding about as if they were having a dance. When they had done the bear said, "Come, let us each tell something he has seen or heard. I'll begin.

"I know a hill where there is a great heap of money. It glitters when the sun shines. If anyone should go there on a sunny day, he would find his fortune."

"I know a town," said the wolf, "where there is no water. Every mouthful has to be brought from a great distance. Now, in the center of that very town, hidden under a stone, where no one can see it, is beautiful pure water. Whoever finds the stone will make a fortune."

"What I can tell is best of all," said the jackal. "I know of a king who has only one daughter, and she lies weak and pale now three long years. If only someone would bathe her in beech leaves she would grow strong and rosy. Whoever cures her will make his fortune."

At the last word day began to dawn. The bear, the wolf, and the jackal left the mill and disappeared into the wood.

The boy had heard it all. Full of thanks he came out of the hopper. "Perhaps," said he to himself, "I may be the one to find the money, take away the stone, and cure the king's daughter. If so, my fortune is sure."

He set forward with a stout heart just as the sun rose. Soon its beams fell on a hill to the right and something glittered in its rays. And here he found the great heap of money, a fortune in itself. Farther on he came to the town where the people had no water. In the center of it there was the stone. He rolled it away, and behold! streams of clear water gushed forth. The people ran to get pitchers and filled them to overflowing. And they gave him a great sum of gold and silver. After this he set out for the kingdom of which the jackal had spoken. When he arrived he asked the king, "What wilt thou give me if I cure thy daughter?"

"If thou canst do this," said the king, "thy fortune is made, for I will give thee my daughter as thy wife."

The youth gathered the beech leaves, the princess bathed in them, and was cured. In great joy the king married the maiden to the youth. So now his fortune was made.

The news of this reached the ears of the selfish brother. He came to his brother and asked how it had all happened. When he heard he said, "I also will go and stay at that mill a night or two." His brother warned him of the danger. But he would not listen. He reached the mill, crept into the hopper, and waited.

As before, at midnight, from some place or other, the bear, the wolf, and the jackal came into the mill, and went leaping and bounding about as if they were having a dance. And when they had done the bear said, "Come, let us each tell something he has seen or heard. I'll begin.

"Next day after I told you my story the money was all taken away."

The wolf said, "And the stone was rolled away and the water found."

"And the king's daughter was cured," added the jackal.

"Then perhaps someone was listening when we talked here," growled the bear.

"Perhaps someone is here now," howled the wolf and the jackal.

"Let us go and look," shrieked the three.

They looked up and down and round about and in all the corners. At last they poked their noses into the hopper. And that was the end of the greedy brother.

But he who had married the king's daughter lived happy ever after and when the king died ruled well and wisely.

—FOLK TALE.

THE WOOING

One morning bright and early a young cock from the next farm stepped into the barnyard where lived a certain young chick.

"Good day, Father Rooster," said he.

"Many thanks, young sir," said Father Rooster.

"I've come a-wooing. May I have your fair daughter Peep for my bride?"

"Ask Mother Hen, Brother Bantam, Sister Cluck, and fair Peep herself; and then we'll see," said Father Rooster.

"Where is Mother Hen?"

"She is sitting in the hay hatching her eggs."

> So away went young cock
>
> With a fly and a leap,
>
> So anxious was he
>
> To marry fair Peep.

"Good day, Mother Hen," said he.

"Many thanks, young sir," said Mother Hen.

"I've come a-wooing. May I have your fair daughter Peep for my bride?"

"Ask Father Rooster, Brother Bantam, Sister Cluck, and fair Peep herself; then we'll see," said Mother Hen.

"Where is Brother Bantam?"

"He's on the gate-post learning to crow."

> So away went young cock
>
> With a fly and a leap,
>
> So anxious was he
>
> To marry fair Peep.

"Good day, Brother Bantam," said he.

"Many thanks," said the other.

"I've come a-wooing. May I have your fair sister Peep for my bride?"

"Ask Father Rooster, Mother Hen, Sister Cluck, and fair Peep herself; then we'll see," said Brother Bantam.

"Where is Sister Cluck?"

"She's with fair Peep."

"And where is fair Peep?"

"She's with Sister Cluck."

> Well, away went young cock
>
> With a fly and a leap,
>
> So anxious was he
>
> To marry fair Peep.

And when he came to two very close together, he said to one, "Good day, Sister Cluck."

And one answered, "Many thanks, young sir."

"I've come a-wooing. May I have your fair sister Peep for my bride?"

"Ask Father Rooster, Mother Hen, Brother Bantam, and fair Peep herself; then we'll see," said Sister Cluck.

"Fair Peep, wilt thou be my bride?" said he. And all the family came up to hear her answer and it wasn't *no*, so it must have been *yes*.

"What hast thou to keep house on?" said Mother Hen to her daughter.

And Brother Bantam answered for her, "A sweet voice;" and Sister Cluck added, "A sweet temper."

>"With these to begin,"
>
>Said Mother Hen,
>
>"There'll be no din."

"What is thy trade, young Master Cock?" asked Father Rooster; "art thou a tailor?"

"Something else for *my* talents."

"A blacksmith?"

"It suits me not."

"Perhaps thou art a watchmaker."

"No, but I'm a time-keeper; I tell people when it is time to rise and go about their work. Is it not a useful trade?"

"That it is.

>"Gladly we give thee fair Peep,
>
>To love and to keep
>
>Safe in thy heart,
>
>Till death do thee part."

>"Then come, thou, sweet wife,
>
>My love and my life,
>
>Step out by my side,

My bonny wee bride."

As they took their way home
They stepped on a tin,
And the tin it bended,
So my story's ended.

—Angela M. Keyes

JACK-THE-GIANT-KILLER

When good King Arthur ruled the land, there lived near Land's End in England, in a place called Cornwall, a farmer who had an only son named Jack. Jack was wide awake and ready of wit, so that nobody and nothing could worst him.

In those days the Mount of Cornwall was kept by a huge giant named Cormoran. He was so fierce and frightful to look at that he was the terror of all the neighboring towns and villages. He lived in a cave in the side of the mount, and whenever he wanted food he waded over to the mainland and took whatever came in his way. At his coming everybody ran away, and then of course he seized the cattle, making nothing of carrying off half-a-dozen oxen on his back at a time, and as for sheep and hogs he tied them around his waist as if they were tallow dips. He had done this for many years, and all Cornwall was in despair.

One day Jack happened to be in the town-hall when the magistrates were sitting in council to think what was best to do.

"What reward," he asked, "will be given to the man who kills Cormoran?"

"He may take the treasure the giant has stored in his cave," they said.

Quoth Jack, "Let me have a try at it."

So he got a horn and shovel and pickaxe. And in the dark of a winter's evening he went over to the mount and fell to work. Before morning he had dug a pit twenty-two feet deep and nearly as broad, and covered it with sticks and straw. Then he strewed a little earth over it so that it looked like plain ground. He then placed himself on the farther side of the pit, and just at the break of day put his horn to his mouth and blew, Tan-tiv-y, Tan-tiv-y!

The noise roused the giant. He rushed out of his cave, crying, "You villain, have you come here to disturb my rest? You shall pay dearly for this. I will take you whole and broil you for breakfast." He had no sooner said this than he tumbled into the pit and made the very foundations of the mount shake.

"Oh, Giant," quoth Jack, "where are you? Has the earth swallowed you up? What do you think now of broiling me for breakfast? Will no other food do than sweet Jack?" Then he gave a most mighty knock with his pickaxe on the very crown of the giant's big head, and killed him on the spot.

Jack then filled up the pit with earth, and went to the cave and took the treasure. When the magistrates heard of Jack's success, they made a law and wrote it on their books that henceforth he should be called

> Jack-the-Giant-Killer,

and they presented him with a sword and belt, and on the belt they wrote these words,

> "Here's the right valiant Cornish man
>
> Who slew the giant Cormoran."

—English Folk Tale

THE PIXIES' THANKS

Once upon a time, and a long time ago, and a long, long time before that, a little old woman had a garden. And in this garden she planted a beautiful bed of tulips. The slim green stalks of them stood in the earth, tall and straight. And every other row of lovely cups they held was red and every other was yellow. At twilight the little old woman patted down the last of them, and went in to boil the kettle for her tea.

Now, as soon as she was gone there came peeping and tripping from the field near by a crowd of pixies. They ran between the rows, and skipped from one flower to the next, and put their slender fingers down into the cups, and clapped their fairy palms together and cried, "How lovely!" But the little old woman drinking her tea before the fire didn't hear a word.

Well, night came, and the pixies' teeny weeny bits of elfin babies grew sleepy. They must have bawled, though of course big ears like yours and mine couldn't have heard them, for all of a sudden all the little pixies scampered home, crying,

> "Coming,

My teeny one,

Coming,

My weeny one,

Watch glowworm

Bright,

My speck of delight!"

And then the cleverest little pixie mother among them thought of something. "Let's lay them in those lovely cradles," said she; "they'll be as safe as a bug in a rose while we are greeting the queen." She at once picked up her baby and ran back with it to the garden. And so did the others with theirs. They laid the tiny babies in the tulip cups and sang them to rest. The tulips rocked to and fro in the wind and made music for the lullaby. The little old woman washing her teacup caught a note of the music and singing, and stopped her clatter to listen, it was so sweet.

As soon as the elfin babies were fast asleep, the pixies tripped lightly off on the very tiptop tips of their toes. The silver Moon was rising, and they were just in time to form a ring on the green and dance in her honor. They circled nine times and then looked up at her, and she beamed down on them and they bowed low. Then she passed on through the heavens to make way for the day.

It was now the dawn of morning. The pixies ran back to the tulip cradles in the little old woman's garden, crying,

"Weeny

Sleepy head,

Leave

Dewy bed,

Time

To get up

From

Soft tulip

Cup."

The little old woman awoke in the nick of time to hear them kissing and caressing the elfin babies as they carried them home. In a bound she was out of bed and at the window, but they had vanished.

For all that she knew they had been there. She could tell it by the tulips. The slim green stalks of them stood in the earth, as they had when she planted them, tall and straight. And every other row of lovely cups they held was red and every other was yellow. Yet there was a wonderful change. It wasn't only the shining drops of dew on them. No, it was something more wonderful—it was fairy fragrance. Every tulip smelled as sweet as a rose. This was the pixies' thanks to the little old woman.

News of these rare tulips went far and wide, and people came from here, there, and everywhere to buy them. So for the rest of her days the little old woman had plenty of money for many a cup of tea, and a pinch of snuff into the bargain.

—Angela M. Keyes

THE CAT AND THE PARROT

Once there was a cat and once there was a parrot. They agreed to invite each other to dinner, turn and turn about. The cat should ask the parrot to-day, and the parrot should ask the cat to-morrow.

Well, it was the cat's turn first. The cat went to market and bought nothing but a pennyworth of rice. The parrot could make no dinner on this meager fare. And what is more, the cat was so ill-mannered that he actually made the parrot cook the food himself. Of course the parrot was too well-bred to complain.

Next day came the parrot's turn. He went to market and bought a leg of meat and a whole fish, head and tail and all, and about thirty pounds of flour, and a tub of butter, and great bunches of luscious grapes. And before his guest came he cooked the food. He made heaps and heaps of brown, crisp spice cakes, thick with currants, oh, enough to fill a washerwoman's basket.

Well, the cat came, and the parrot set the whole meal before him, keeping only two cakes for himself. The cat ate the meat till he licked the plate, and he picked the fish till the bones were clean, and he sucked the grapes till the skins were dry, and then he began on the cakes; and he ate the whole basketful. Then he looked up at the parrot and said, "Have you any more?"

"Take my two cakes," said the parrot. And the cat took them. Then he looked up at the parrot and said, "Have you any more?"

This was too much for the parrot. Bristling his feathers, he said sharply, "There's nothing left but me." And the cat looked him over, licked his chops, and—gullup, gulloo—down went the parrot, bones, beak, and feathers.

Now an old woman had seen it all, and she was so shocked she picked up a stone, and cried, "You unnatural cat, how could you eat your friend the parrot? Scat! away with you, before I hit you with this stone."

"Old woman," said the cat, "I've eaten a basketful of cakes, I've eaten my friend the parrot, and shall I blush to eat an old hag like you? No, surely not." And—gullup, gulloo—down went the old woman with the stone in her hand.

Then the cat walked along the road till he met a man beating a donkey to make him go. "Cat," cried the man, "get out of the way, or my donkey may kick you."

"Man," said the cat, "I've eaten a basketful of cakes, I've eaten my friend the parrot, I've eaten an old woman, and shall I blush to eat a miserable donkey driver? No, surely not." And—gullup, gulloo—down went the man and his donkey.

After this the cat walked on again till he met a wedding procession. At the head came the king with his newly made bride, and behind him marched a company of soldiers, and behind them tramped ever and ever so many elephants, two and two, and two and two, and two and two, and a great many more.

"Cat," said the happy king, kindly, "turn out of the road a little, or my elephants may trample you to death."

"King," said the cat, "you don't know me. I've eaten a basketful of cakes, I've eaten my friend the parrot, I've eaten a miserable man and his donkey, and shall I blush to eat a beggarly king? No, surely not." And—gullup, gulloo—down went the king, down went the queen, down went the soldiers, bayonets and all, down went the elephants, two and two and two and two.

After this the cat walked on more slowly, for he was somewhat heavy. On the way two landcrabs went scuttling across the road. "Run away, run away, Pussycat," they squeaked, "or we might nip you."

"Ha, ha, ha!" laughed the cat, shaking his fat sides. "Ho, ho, ho!" he roared, showing his teeth; "you don't know me. I've eaten a basketful of cakes, I've eaten my friend the parrot, I've eaten a miserable man and his donkey, I've eaten a king and his bride, I've eaten a company of soldiers, I've eaten a herd of elephants, two and two, and shall I blush to eat two silly little landcrabs? Nay, not so." And he pounced upon the landcrabs, gullup, gulloo, gulloo, gullup, in two swallows they were inside the cat.

But—when their eyes were used to the darkness, the landcrabs made out the king sitting with his head in his hands, very unhappy. Across his knee lay the newly made bride in a dead faint. Near them the company of soldiers were trying to form fours. Behind these the elephants were trumpeting, the donkey was braying, the parrot was whetting his beak on his own claws, and the old woman was scolding the cat roundly. In a corner they made out a great pile of cakes.

The landcrabs said, "His sides are soft: let's get out." Nip, nip, they went, nip, nip, nip. And out they scuttled. Then out walked the king with his bride on his arm, out marched the soldiers, out tramped the elephants, two and two, out went the man and his donkey without any beating, out hobbled the old woman, and out flew the parrot.

And the cat had to spend a night and a day sewing up his sides.

—Eastern Folk Tale

LAMPBLACK

A poor black paint lay very unhappy in its tube. It had tumbled out of an artist's color-box and had lain unnoticed for a year. "I am only Lampblack," he said to himself. "The master never looks at me: he says I am heavy, dull, lusterless, useless. I wish I could cake and dry up and die, as poor Flakewhite did."

But Lampblack could not die; he could only lie in his tin tube and pine, like a silly, sorrowful thing as he was, in company with some broken bits of charcoal and a rusty palette-knife. The master never touched him; month after month passed by, and he was never thought of; the other paints had all their turn of fair fortune, and went out into the world to great halls and mighty palaces, transfigured and rejoicing in a thousand beautiful shapes and services. But Lampblack was always passed over as dull and coarse. Indeed he knew himself to be so, poor fellow, and this made it all the worse. "You are only a deposit!" said the other colors to him; and he felt that it was disgraceful to be a deposit, though he was not quite sure what it meant.

"If only I were happy like the others!" thought poor, sooty Lampblack, sorrowful in his corner. "There is Bistre, now, he is not so very much better-looking than I am, and yet they can do nothing without him, whether it is a girl's face or a wimple in a river!"

The others were all so happy in this beautiful bright studio, where the open casements were hung with green myrtle, and where the silence was filled with the singing of nightingales. Cobalt, with a touch or two, became the loveliness of summer skies at morning; the Lakes and Carmines bloomed in a thousand exquisite flowers and fancies; the Chromes and Ochres (mere dull earths) were allowed to spread themselves in sheets of gold that took the shine of the sun into the darkest places; Umber, a somber and gloomy thing, could lurk in a child's curls and laugh in a child's smiles; whilst all the families of the Vermilions, the Blues, the Greens, lived in a perpetual glory of sunset or sunrise, of ocean waves or autumn woods, of kingly pageant or of martial pomp.

It was very hard. Poor Lampblack felt as if his very heart would break, above all when he thought of pretty little Rose Madder, whom he loved dearly, and who never would even look at him, she was so proud, because she was always placed in nothing less than rosy clouds, or the hearts of roses, or something as fair and spiritual.

"I am only a wretched deposit!" sighed Lampblack, and the rusty palette-knife grumbled back, "My own life has been ruined in cleaning dirty brushes!"

"But at least you were of use once; but I never am,—never!" said Lampblack. And indeed he had been there so long that the spiders had spun their silver fleeces all about him, and he was growing as gray as an old bottle does in a dark cellar.

At that moment the door of the studio opened, and there came a flood of light, and the step of a man was heard; the hearts of all the colors jumped for joy. It was their magician, who out of mere common clays and ground ores could raise them at a touch into splendors immortal.

Only the heart of poor dusty Lampblack did not beat a throb the more, because he was always left alone and never was thought worthy of even a glance. But he could not believe his senses when the master crossed the floor to the dark corner where he lay under the spiders' webs. Lampblack felt sick and faint with rapture. Had his turn come at last?

The master took him up. "You will do for this work," he said; and Lampblack was borne trembling to an easel. The colors, for once neglected, crowded together to watch, looking in their bright tin tubes like rows of little soldiers in armor.

"It is dull Old Deposit," they murmured to one another, and felt contemptuous, but curious, as scornful people often will be.

"I am going to be glorious and great," thought Lampblack, and his heart swelled high; for nevermore would they be able to hurl the name of Deposit at him, a name which hurt all the more because he did not know what it meant.

"You will do for this work," said the master, and let Lampblack out of his metal prison-house into the light and touched him with the brush that was the wand of magic.

"What am I going to be?" wondered Lampblack, as he felt himself taken on to a large piece of deal board, so large that he felt he must be going to make at the least the outline of an athlete or the shadows of a tempest.

He could not tell what he was becoming; but he was happy enough and grand enough only to be used. He began to dream a thousand things of all the scenes he would be in, and all the hues that he would wear, and all the praise that he would hear when he went out into that wonderful world where his master was so much admired.

But he was harshly roused from his secret dreams; all the colors were laughing and tittering round him till the little tin helmets they wore shook with their merriment.

"Old Deposit is going to be a sign-post," they cried to one another so merrily that the spiders, who are not companionable creatures, came to the doors of their dens to chuckle too. A sign-post! Lampblack, stretched out in joy upon the board, roused himself and gazed at the change. He had been made into seven letters, thus:

BANDITA.

This word in the Italian country, where the English painter's studio was, means, Do not trespass, Do not shoot, Do not show yourself here: anything, indeed, that is uncivil to all comers. In these seven letters, outspread upon the board, was Lampblack disgraced!

Farewell, hopes and dreams! He had been employed to paint a sign-board, a thing stoned by the boys, blown on by the winds, gnawed by the rats, and drenched with the winter's rains. Better the dust and the cobwebs of his old corner than such shame as this!

But there was no help for it. He was dried with a drench of turpentine, hastily clothed in a coat of copal, and, ere he yet was fully aware of all his misery, was being borne away upon the great board out of doors and handed to the gardener. It was the master himself who did this to him. As the door closed on him, he heard all the colors laughing, and the laugh of little Rose Madder was highest of all as she cried to Naples Yellow, who was a dandy and made court to her, "Poor old ugly Deposit! He will grumble to the owls and the bats now!"

The door shut him out forever from all the joyous company and the palace of beauty, and the rough hands of the gardener grasped him and carried him to the edge of the garden, where the wall overlooked the public road, and there fastened him up on high with a band of iron round the trunk of a tree.

That night it rained heavily, the north wind blew, and there was thunder. Lampblack, out in the storm without his tin house to shelter him, felt that of all creatures wretched on the face of the earth there was not one so miserable as he. A sign-board! Nothing but a sign-board!

A color, created for art and artists, could not feel more grievously disgraced. Oh, how he longed for his tin tube and the quiet nook with the charcoal and the palette-knife! He had been unhappy there indeed, but he had had some sort of hope to comfort him,—some chance still remaining that one day he might be allowed to be at least the shadow of some immortal work. Now—nevermore could he be anything but what he was; change there could be none till weather and time should have done their work on him, and he be rotting on the wet earth, a shattered and worm-eaten wreck.

Day broke,—a gloomy, misty morning.

From where he was disgraced upon the tree-trunk he could no longer even see his beloved home, the studio; he could see only a dusky, intricate tangle of branches all about him, and below the wall of flint, with the Banksia that grew on it, and the hard muddy highway, drenched with the storm of the night.

A man passed in a miller's cart, and stood up and scowled at him, because the people had liked to come and shoot and trap the birds of the master's wooded gardens, and they knew that they must not do it now. A slug crawled over him, and a snail also. A woodpecker hammered at him with its strong beak. A boy went by under the wall, and threw stones at him, and called him names. The rain poured down again heavily. He thought of the happy painting-room, where it had seemed always summer and always sunshine, and where now in the forenoon all the colors were marshaling in the pageantry of the Arts, as he had seen them do hundreds of times from his lonely corner. All the misery of the past looked happiness now.

"If I were only dead, like Flakewhite," he thought; but the stones only bruised, they did not kill him; and the iron band only hurt, it did not stifle him. For whatever suffers very much, has much strength to continue to exist. His loyal heart almost hated the master who had brought him to such a fate as this.

The day grew apace, and noon went by, and with it the rain passed. The sun shone out once more, and Lampblack, even imprisoned and wretched as he was, could not but see how beautiful the wet leaves looked, and the gossamers all hung with rain-drops, and the blue sky that shone through the boughs; for he had not lived with an artist all his days to be blind, even in pain, to the loveliness of nature. Some little brown birds tripped out too with the sun—very simple and plain in their dress, but Lampblack knew they were the loves of the poets, for he had heard the master call them so many times in summer nights. The little brown birds came tripping and pecking about on the grass underneath his tree-trunk, and then flew on the top of the wall, which was covered with Banksia and many other creepers. The brown birds sang a little song, for though they sing most in the moonlight they do sing by day too, and sometimes all day long. And what they sang was this:

"Oh, how happy we are, how happy!

No nets dare now be spread for us,

No cruel boys dare climb,

And no cruel shooters fire.

We are safe, quite safe,

And the sweet summer has begun!"

Lampblack listened, and even in his misery was soothed by the tender liquid sounds that these little throats poured out among the bloom of the Banksia flowers. And when one of the brown birds came and sat on a branch by him, swaying itself and drinking the rain-drops off a leaf, he ventured to ask, as well as he could for the iron that strangled him, why they were so safe, and what made them so happy.

The bird looked at him in surprise.

"Do you not know?" he said. "It is you!"

"I!" echoed Lampblack, and could say no more, for he feared that the bird was mocking him, a poor, silly, rusty black paint, only spread out to rot in fair weather and foul. What good could he do to any creature?

"You," repeated the nightingale. "Did you not see that man under the wall? He had a gun; we should have been dead but for you. We will come and sing to you all night long, as you like it; and when we go to bed at dawn, I will tell my cousins, the thrushes and merles, to take our places, so that you shall hear somebody singing near you all day long."

Lampblack was silent. His heart was too full to speak. Was it possible that he was of use, after all.

"Can it be true?" he said, timidly.

"Quite true," said the nightingale.

"Then the master knew best," thought Lampblack.

The colors in the studio had all the glories of the world, but he was of use in it, after all; he could save these little lives. He was poor and despised, bruised by stones and drenched by storms; yet was he content, for he had not been made quite in vain.

The sunset poured its red and golden splendors through the darkness of the boughs, and the birds sang all together, shouting for joy and praising God.

—LA RAMÉE

LAZY JACK

Once upon a time there was a boy whose name was Jack. His mother was very poor, but she was hard-working and tried to get her living by spinning. Jack was so lazy he never did anything to help her. So, at last, she said that he should not eat his porridge unless he earned it.

At this out shuffled Jack and hired himself to a farmer and got for his day's labor a shining new penny. Home he went with it, but on the way let it slip out of his fingers into a brook, unknown to himself.

When his mother saw him smiling and holding his fist closed, she said, "Well, Jack, did you earn your porridge to-day?"

"That I did, mother," said Jack, "and here's the penny." With that he opened his empty hand.

"A penny," cried his mother, in high delight, "give it here, my darling boy." But when she saw the empty hand she changed her tune. "You stupid lout," said she, "you've lost the good money. That's no way to bring home a penny. The safest thing to do with a penny is to put it into your pocket and come straight home."

"Say no more about it, sweet mother," whimpered Jack, "that's what I'll do the next time." So his mother gave him his supper.

The next day Jack went out again, and this time hired himself to a cowherd and got for his day's labor a jug of new milk. Jack took the jug, squeezed it into the largest pocket of his coat, and set off home, spilling the milk at every step, so that by the time he got home there wasn't a drop left.

When his mother saw his pocket bulging out, she asked, "What have you there, Jack, my son?"

"A jug of new milk, mother," answered Jack, tugging it out of his pocket.

"A jug of new milk," cried his mother, "and you've spilled it! Have you no sense, you ninny-hammer? That's no way to bring home a jug of milk. The safest way to carry a jug of milk is to put it on your head and hold it with both hands and come straight home."

"Say no more about it, sweet mother," whimpered Jack, beginning to blubber; "that's what I'll do the next time." So his mother gave him his supper that time, too.

Well, the next day Jack hired himself to a farmer, and got for his day's labor a fine fresh cream cheese. Jack took that cheese, placed it on his head, held it down firmly with both hands, and set out home. Now, Jack's head was warm and the cheese was soft. So it wasn't long before it began to get softer. By the time he reached home part of it had oozed down over his face and more of it had matted into his hair; he was a sight to behold.

When his mother saw him, she threw up her arms and cried, "Dearie me, dearie me, whatever has happened to my own bonny son?"

"Why, nothing, mother," said Jack, "and see the fine cheese I've brought you home." With that he took down from his head a bit of grease in each hand.

"You've spoiled a cheese, a fine cream cheese," screamed his mother. "Have you no sense at all, at all, in your empty head, you numbskull? That's no way to bring home a cheese. The safest thing to do with a cheese is to take it in both hands, hold it out before you, and come straight home."

"Say no more about it, sweet mother," said Jack, beginning to snuffle, "that's what I'll do the next time."

So he didn't go supperless to bed that night either.

It was a baker Jack hired himself to the next day, and at the close of it the baker gave him a cat. "Your mother will find her a good mouser," said he. And Jack said, "Thank you, kindly, sir," and took the cat. He held her with both hands out before him and started straight for home. On the way a mouse scurried across his path and the cat leaped from his hands; but Jack still held them out, ready for her when she should come back, and kept on toward home.

When he reached home his mother looked at his hands and said, "What have you in your hands, Jack?"

"I had a cat, mother," said he, "a good mouser, but she made after a mouse and hasn't come back yet."

"Get out of my sight," cried his mother, "before I lose my patience and do something I might be sorry for. Haven't you an atom of sense about you at all, at all, at all? Wouldn't a child know that's no way to bring home a live cat? The safest thing to do with a cat is to tie a string around her neck, put her on the ground, and draw her home after you."

"Say no more about it, sweet mother," cried Jack, bawling outright; "that's what I'll do the very next time." So his mother wouldn't see him starve that night.

Well, the very next day Jack hired out to a butcher, and got for his day's labor a splendid shoulder of mutton for Sunday's dinner, for this was Saturday. Jack took the mutton, tied a string around it, put it on the ground, and dragged it home after him in the mud and dirt. So by the time he got home the meat was completely ruined.

When his mother saw it she was so upset that she threw her apron over her head and rocked herself to and fro and wept aloud. "If you had the least grain of sense in you, you useless omadhaun," she wailed, "you'd have brought the sweet meat home on your shoulder."

Jack put his arms around his mother and kissed her and promised to do that the next time. So she gave him his supper, but they had to make their Sunday dinner of cabbage.

Monday morning, bright and early, Jack went out once more and hired himself to a cattle-drover and for his day's labor got a donkey. Although Jack was a husky fellow, he found it hard to hoist the donkey on his shoulder, but mindful of his mother's grief he got it up and set out home slowly with the prize.

Now it chanced that on the way home he had to pass the house of a beautiful girl who unfortunately was deaf and dumb. The doctors said she would never speak until someone should make her laugh. Many had tried but without success. In despair her father, who was very rich, had promised that very day whoever could make her laugh should marry her.

The girl happened to be looking out of the window when Jack came along with the donkey on his shoulders, its legs sticking up in the air. He looked so funny she burst into a merry fit of laughter, and at once was able to hear and speak.

So her father, overjoyed, gave her to Jack with a sackful of money and more to come.

"My love, your fortune is made," cried his mother, when she heard the good news. And she went to live with Jack and his bride, and they all had plenty and were happy ever after.

>Ting-a-ling-a-ling,
>
>Let the wedding bells ring.

—Folk Tale

THE TIME THAT WILL COME AGAIN

One warm bright day in autumn, when the whole world was changing to brown and red and gold, a little squealing pig was sent by his mother to bring home some beechnuts to Piggikin, the baby.

"They're dropping now, tender and sweet, in the wood," said Mother Sow. "Off with you and get some." So

>With a run and a squeal
>
>Away went the pig,
>
>With an odd little reel.

Now, on the way he passed a boy and a girl sitting by the roadside, with their backs to him. And the boy was saying to the girl,

>"A long time ago when pigs had wings
>
>And pups grew in the tree-tops,
>
>In that good time donkeys brayed in rhyme
>
>And fiddles danced the barn hops"—

"That's very strange," said the pig; "can it be true? I'll ask the old witch owl about it. I'd like a pair of wings; I'd fly high, I can tell you." So

>With a run and a squeal

> Away went the pig,
>
> With an odd little reel;

and he left the path to the wood to make for a barn half a mile off, where the old witch owl lived.

On the way he met a pup whose father had told him to guard the kennel while he himself went in search of a bone. The pup was rolling on the ground in the sunshine.

"O roly-poly pup," called out the pig, "what do you think I heard this morning?"

"What?" said the roly-poly pup, running away from the kennel.

> "A long time ago when pigs had wings
>
> And pups grew in the tree-tops,
>
> In that good time
>
> Donkeys brayed in rhyme
>
> And fiddles danced the barn hops."

"That's very strange," said the pup; "can it be true? We'll ask the old witch owl about it. I'd like to grow in a tree-top. I'd see farther than my nose, I can tell you." So

> With a run and a squeal
>
> Away went the pig with an odd little reel
>
> And the roly-poly pup followed after.

Well, on the way they met a donkey kicking his heels to get rid of the pack on his back. And they called out to him, "O kicking, kicking donkey, what do you think we heard this very morning?"

"What?" said the kicking, kicking donkey, as he kicked the pack from his back.

> "A long time ago when pigs had wings
>
> And pups grew in the tree-tops,
>
> In that good time donkeys brayed in rhyme
>
> And fiddles danced the barn hops."

"That's very strange," said the donkey; "can it be true? We'll ask the old witch owl about it. I'd like to bray in rhyme. I'd bring down the house, I can tell you." So

>With a run and a squeal
>
>Away went the pig with an odd little reel,
>
>And the roly-poly pup and the kicking, kicking donkey followed after.

Halfway to the barn they met a fiddle lying near a bench. He was in such a bad temper that he had broken the string that makes the sweetest music. But the others were too full of their news to notice his ill humor.

"O fiddle diddle," they cried, "what do you think we heard this very morning?"

"What?" snapped the fiddle, and he broke another string.

>"A long time ago when pigs had wings
>
>And pups grew in the tree-tops,
>
>In that good time donkeys brayed in rhyme,
>
>And fiddles danced the barn hops."

"What nonsense!" growled the fiddle, in such an ugly tone that even the donkey rose on his hind legs to cover his big ears with his forefeet.

"We're going to ask the old witch owl about it," said the pup. "Come along and hear what she says."

"Rr-r-r-r-zing, you silly thing," snarled the fiddle, so fiercely that without waiting for more,

>With a run and a squeal
>
>Away went the pig with an odd little reel,
>
>And the roly-poly pup and the kicking, kicking donkey,
>
>And the ill-tempered fiddle followed after.

He sneaked along, though, behind the others, and tripped often in his broken strings, and this made his temper worse.

Well, the day was darkening into twilight when they reached the barn. But they were so anxious to hear the old witch owl's opinion that they didn't notice this. The old witch owl stood in a little round opening in the front of the barn, high up near the pointed top where the weathercock turns. She was looking out into the gathering darkness, planning her voyage into the night.

"There she is," squealed the pig in a whisper, getting behind the pup.

"Her ears are bigger than mine," said the donkey, getting behind the pig.

But the fiddle pushed to the front and growled, "Rr-r-r-r-zing, you silly thing, I'm not afraid of an old witch owl. I'll ask the ridiculous question."

"Do, sweet fiddle," whispered the little squealing pig and the roly-poly pup and the kicking, kicking donkey, "how kind of you to have come."

"Rr-r-r-r-zing, you silly thing, and you, and you; I came to please myself."

"Madame Witch Owl," he growled, spoiling the music of the verse, "is it true that

"A long time ago pigs had wings

And pups grew in the tree-tops,

In that good time donkeys brayed in rhyme,

And fiddles danced the barn hops?"

The old witch looked down at him. And her eyes glowed so much like two round wheels of fire that the fiddle in secret fright burst another string. But for all that he stared back at her. "Hoot-hoot-hoot," she cried, "wait till I've heard your betters. Let the pig stand forth and the pup and the donkey."

Out came the little squealing pig, but not very far, so that the roly-poly pup might catch him by the tail in case of need; and out came the roly-poly pup, but not very far, so that the little squealing pig might catch him by the tail in case of need; and out came the kicking, kicking donkey, but not very far, so that he might get behind the pup and the pig in case of need.

"Pig, pig," said the old witch owl, "how did you hear this?"

And the little pig began in a squealing little voice to tell her how Mother Sow had sent him to the wood to get some beechnuts for Piggikin, the baby, and how he had heard the boy tell it to the girl, and how he had set off to ask her about it.

"And Piggikin is still hungry for the beechnuts, is he?" asked the old witch owl, looking beyond the little pig into the darkness.

"Yes," said the little pig, in a very little voice.

"And Mother Sow is getting anxious as the night grows darker."

"The night," cried the little squealing pig and the roly-poly pup and the kicking, kicking donkey, drawing nearer together. And they looked fearfully over their shoulders as the shadows of the apple-tree near the barn moved nearer to them.

When the old witch owl brought back her eyes from the darkness, she looked at the roly-poly pup, and he went on to tell, in a very loud voice to give himself courage, how his father had left him to guard the kennel, but how when he heard the news he, too, set off to ask her about it.

"And the kennel is still unguarded, is it?" asked the old witch owl, looking beyond the roly-poly pup into the darkness.

"Yes," said the roly-poly pup, in a very small voice.

"And Father Dog is getting anxious as the night grows darker."

"The night," cried the roly-poly pup and the kicking, kicking donkey and the little squealing pig, drawing nearer together. And they looked fearfully over their shoulders as the shadows of the apple-tree near the barn moved nearer to them.

When the old witch owl brought her eyes back from the darkness she looked at the kicking, kicking donkey, and he straightway began to roar how his master had given him a pack to carry, but how, when he heard the news, he had kicked it off and set out to ask her about it.

When he finished he joined forepaws with the pig and the pup and danced around the fiddle; the pig singing,

"O for a pair of wings to fly high,"

and the pup singing,

"O to grow in a tree-top and see farther than my nose,"

and the donkey singing,

"O to bray in rhyme and bring down the house."

And then they all sang together,

"O for the time when pigs had wings

And pups grew in the tree-tops,

In that good time donkeys brayed in rhyme,

And fiddles danced the barn hops."

The fiddle never even noticed them; he still stared at the old witch owl, though he did not dare to say anything.

"You kicked off the pack, did you?" asked the old witch owl, turning the full blaze of her eyes on the donkey.

"Yes," he gasped, running behind the pup and the pig, and the pig tried to catch the pup by the tail, and the pup tried to catch the pig by the tail.

"Do you think," she cried in a frightful voice, and her feathers stood out straight around her, "that runaways and idlers will ever fly high or see farther than their noses or bring music into the world? They bring nothing but sorrow, sorrow to those that love them." And suddenly the old witch owl looked out into the night and called,

"Hoo-oo-oo-oo. Is it you-oo-oo? Is it you-oo-oo?"

Immediately out of the night walked the mother of the squealing pig and the father of the roly-poly pup and the master of the kicking, kicking donkey. And into the sky came the moon. And into the moonlight trooped crowds of boys and girls from the land of dreams, led by the boy and girl the little pig had passed in the morning, more and more of them, till they surrounded the barn and covered the shadows cast by the apple-tree.

The little squealing pig ran to his mother and the roly-poly pup ran to his father and the kicking, kicking donkey ran to his master; and there was great rejoicing. The donkey begged his master for a beating, saying he richly deserved it, and so did the pup and the pig. But the grown-ups said, "They'll do better next time."

When the dream children heard this they streamed out into the moonlight back to their dreams, singing,

> "The time will come again when pigs will have wings
>
> And pups will grow in the tree-tops,
>
> In that good time donkeys will bray in rhyme,
>
> And fiddles will dance the barn hops."

And lo and behold! when the fiddle heard them he felt his ill-humor slipping away. And as the old witch owl looked at them his strings mended themselves.

Dancing down the path and out into the moonlight after the children he sounded his sweetest notes in time to their singing; and the little pig and his mother and the roly-poly pup and his father and the donkey and his master followed and took up the children's song. To the very end of it the fiddle danced and played his merriest. At the turn of the road he looked back at the old witch owl and she was looking at him.

"The little pig's news is good," he cried,

"I'm off to spread it far and wide."

And as she sailed off into the night he was sure she nodded at him.

And Piggikin got the nuts after all, though they were a day late.

—Angela M. Keyes

THE OWL'S ANSWER TO TOMMY

One evening Tommy's grandmother had been telling him and his little brother Johnny a story about a brownie who used to do all the work in a neighbor's house before the family got up in the morning. But the maids caught sight of him one night, and they felt so sorry to see his ragged coat that the next night they laid near his bowl of bread and milk a new suit and a new linen shirt. Brownie put the things on and danced around the room, singing,

"What have we here? Hemten hamten!

Here will I nevermore tread nor stampen."

And away he danced through the door and never came back again. Tommy wanted to know why, but his grandmother couldn't tell him. "The Old Owl knows," she said, "I don't. Ask her."

Now Tommy was a lazy boy. He thought that if only he could find a brownie that would do his work he would save himself a great deal of trouble. So that night, while little Johnnie lay sound asleep beside him, in the loft of the kitchen, as rosy and rosier than an apple, he lay broad awake, thinking of his grandmother's story. "There's an owl living in the old shed by the lake," he thought. "It may be the Old Owl herself, and she knows, Granny says. When father's gone to bed and the moon rises, I'll go and ask her."

By and by the moon rose like gold and went up into the heavens like silver, flooding the fields with a pale ghostly light. Tom crept softly down the ladder and stole out. It was a glorious night, though everything but the wind and Tommy seemed asleep. The stones, the walls, the gleaming lanes, were so intensely still, the church tower in the valley seemed awake and watching, but silent; the houses in the village round it had all their eyes shut; and it seemed to Tommy as if the very fields had drawn white sheets over them, and lay sleeping also.

"Hoot! hoot!" said a voice from the fir wood behind him. Somebody else was awake, then. "It's the Old Owl," said Tommy; and there she came swinging heavily across the moor with a flapping stately flight, and sailed into the shed by the lake. The old lady moved faster than she appeared to do, and though Tommy ran hard she was in the shed some time before him. When he got in, no bird was to be seen, but he heard a sound from above, and there sat the Old Owl, blinking at him—Tommy—with yellow eyes.

"Come up, come up!" said she hoarsely. She could speak then! Beyond all doubt it was *the* Old Owl, and none other.

"Come up here! come up here!" said the Old Owl.

Tommy had often climbed up for fun to the beam that ran across the shed where the Old Owl sat. He climbed up now, and sat face to face with her, and thought her eyes looked as if they were made of flame.

"Now, what do you want?" said the Owl.

"Please," said Tommy, "can you tell me where to find the brownies, and how to get one to come and live with us?"

"Oohoo!" said the Owl, "that's it, is it? I know of two brownies."

"Hurrah!" said Tommy. "Where do they live?"

"In your house," said the Owl.

Tommy was aghast.

"In our house!" he exclaimed. "Whereabouts? Let me rummage them out. Why do they do nothing?"

"One of them is too young," said the Owl.

"But why doesn't the other work?" asked Tommy.

"He is idle, he is idle," said the Owl, and she gave herself such a shake as she said it that the fluff went flying through the shed, and Tommy nearly tumbled off the beam in fright.

"Then we don't want him," said he. "What is the use of having brownies if they do nothing to help us? But perhaps if you would tell me where to find them," said Tommy, "I could tell them what to do."

"Could you?" said the Owl. "Oohoo! oohoo!" and Tommy couldn't tell whether she were hooting or laughing.

"Of course I could," he said. "They might be up and sweep the house, and light the fire, and spread the tables, and that sort of thing, before Father came down. The Brownie did all that in Granny's mother's young days. And they might tidy the room, and fetch the turf, and pick up my chips, and sort Granny's scraps. Oh! there's plenty to do."

"So there is," said the Owl. "Oohoo! Well, I can tell you where to find one of the brownies; and if you can find him, he will tell you where his brother is. But all this depends upon whether you feel equal to undertaking it, and whether you will follow my directions."

"I am quite ready to go," said Tommy, "and I will do as you tell me. I feel sure I could persuade them to come; if they only knew how every one would love them if they made themselves useful!"

"Oohoo! oohoo!" said the Owl. "Now listen. You must go to the north side of the lake when the moon is shining—("I know brownies like water," muttered Tommy)—and turn yourself round three times, saying this charm:

'Twist me, and turn me, and show me the Elf—

I looked in the water, and saw—'

When you have got so far look into the water, and think of a word that will rhyme with Elf, and at the same moment you will see the brownie."

"Is the brownie a merman," said Tommy, "that he lives under water?"

"That depends on whether he has a fish's tail," said the Owl, "and that you can see for yourself."

"Well, the moon is shining, so I shall go," said Tommy. "Gooby-by, and thank you, Ma'am;" and he jumped down and went, saying to himself, "I believe he is a merman, all the same, or else how could he live in the lake?"

The moon shone very brightly on the center of the lake. Tommy knew the place well, for there was an Echo there, with whom he had often talked. Round the edges grew rushes and water plants, and turning himself three times, as the Old Owl had told him, he repeated the charm:

"Twist me and turn me and show me the Elf—

I looked in the water and saw—"

Now for it! He looked in, and saw—his own face.

"Why, there's no one there but myself!" said Tommy. "And what can the word be? I must have done it wrong. It cannot be myself."

"Myself!" said the Echo.

Tommy was almost surprised to find the Echo awake at this time of night.

"Much you know about it!" said he. "Belf! Celf! Delf! Felf! Helf! Jelf! There can't be a word to fit it. And then to look for a brownie and see nothing but myself!"

"Myself," said the Echo.

"Will you be quiet?" said Tommy. "If you would tell me the word there would be some meaning in your interference; but to roar 'Myself!' at me, which neither rhymes nor runs—it does rhyme, though, as it happens," he added; "how very odd! it runs too—

'Twist me and turn me and show me the Elf—

I looked in the water and saw myself,'—

which I certainly did. What can it mean? The Old Owl knows, as Granny would say; so I shall go back and ask her."

And back he went. There sat the Old Owl as before.

"Oohoo!" said she, as Tommy climbed up. "What did you see in the lake?"

"I saw nothing but myself," said Tommy, indignantly.

"And what did you expect to see?" asked the Owl.

"I expected to see a brownie," said Tommy; "you told me."

"And what are brownies like, pray?" inquired the Owl.

"The one Granny knew was a useful little fellow, something like a man," said Tommy.

"Ah!" said the Owl, "but you know at present this one is an idle little fellow, something like a little man. Oohoo! oohoo! Good night, or rather, good morning, for it is long past midnight." And the old lady began to shake her feathers for a start. "Stay," said she, "I think I had better take you home."

"I know the way, thank you," said Tommy.

"Do as I say," said the Owl. "Lean your full weight against me and shut your eyes."

Tommy laid his head against the Owl's feathers. Down he sank and sank. He jumped up with a start to save himself, opened his eyes, and found that he was sitting in the loft with Johnnie sleeping by his side.

"Get up, Johnnie, I've a story to tell you," he cried. And he told Johnnie all about it.

And after that Tommy and Johnnie were the most useful little brownies in that whole country.

—From Mrs. Ewing's Brownies

THE STORY OF COQUERICO

Hear the story of this one.

He was a queer-looking little creature. He came out in the brood of a handsome black Spanish hen. All his brothers and sisters were as pretty as you would see in a day's walk, but he was very odd-looking. He had only one good eye, one good wing, and one good leg to carry him about, hippety-hop, hippety-hop. When his mother saw he was crippled, she at once loved him best, and gave him the splendid name of Coquerico. But hear about him.

Maybe you think a one-eyed, one-armed, one-legged chick like Coquerico would be good and gentle. Why, if one of his brothers ran against him without meaning to, Coquerico flew at the poor fellow and called him names. And he was so conceited that he thought himself better than his brothers and sisters, and that he knew more than his mother.

So one day he hippety-hopped up to his mother and said, "My lady mother, I am too good for this family; I should be in the king's court. I'm off to Madrid, where the king lives."

"What are you thinking of, my poor little one?" cried his mother. "Who has put such nonsense into your head? Where would my little crippled one find a home like this—mulberry trees to shade him, a white-washed henroost, a high dunghill, worms and corn in plenty, brothers and sisters that are fond of him, and a mother who loves him dearly. Stay where you are, my child; believe me I know what is best for you."

"Do you think so?" said Coquerico, saucily. "I don't. I wish to go out into the world, where everyone may hear of me, I am so clever. I'm off to Madrid to see the king."

"But, my son, have you never looked in the brook?" asked his mother. "Don't you know that you have only one eye, one wing, and one leg? To make your way in the world you need the sharp eyes of a fox, the swift wings of a hawk, and the many soft legs of a spider. Once outside, you are lost."

"My good mother," said Coquerico, just as saucily, "I am well able to take care of myself. I am better than my family and must find people who can see how clever I am. So I'm off to Madrid to see the king."

"Well, my son," said the anxious mother-hen, "listen to your mother's last words. Keep away from people known as cooks and scullions; you will know them by their paper caps, tucked up sleeves, and great sharp knives."

So away went Coquerico, making believe not to see the tear in his mother's eye. Without caring for those he left, he hippety-hopped out the gate and stopped only long enough to crow three times, "Cock-a-doodle-doo!" Then over the fields he went hippety-hop, hippety-hop.

By and by he came to a small brook almost choked by a couple of dead leaves. "My friend," it called out to him, "will you free me that I may flow on? One stroke of your beak is enough."

"Do I look like a brook-sweeper?" answered Coquerico. "Help yourself; I'm off to Madrid to see the king." And on he went, hippety-hop, hippety-hop.

A little farther on Coquerico saw the wind lying breathless on the ground. "Dear friend, help me," it cried; "here on earth we should help one another. If you will fan me a little with your wing I shall have strength to rise to my place among the clouds, where I am needed for the next whirlwind."

"Do I look like a wind-bellows," answered Coquerico; "help yourself. I am off to Madrid to see the king." And on he went, hippety-hop, hippety-hop.

A little farther on he came to a newly mown field, where the farmers had piled up the weeds to burn them. As he stopped his hippety-hop to search among a smoking heap for a kernel of corn, he saw a little flame, barely flickering, it was so nearly out.

"My dear friend," cried the flame, faintly, "will you bring me a few dry straws to rekindle me that I may burn brightly?"

"Do I look like a servant?" cried Coquerico, haughtily; "I'll teach you to call out to a fowl that has business with the king." And he leaped on the heap of dried weeds and trampled it down till it smothered the flame! Then he flapped his one wing and crowed three times, "Cock-a-doodle-doo," as if he had done something to be proud of.

And so strutting and crowing, though he had to go hippety-hop, he arrived at Madrid and the king's palace. Grand and beautiful as it was, he did not stop to look at it, but made for the hen yard, stopping every second step to crow, "Cock-a-doodle," to tell the king and all the world he was coming.

In the hen yard there was of course no king, but a boy with a paper cap on his head and sleeves tucked up and a great sharp knife in his hand. "A scullion, I suppose," said Coquerico to himself, "but he will not stop me; I have business with the king."

"Well, you're an odd one," cried the boy, coming over to look at the newcomer. "Cook wants a rare bird for the king's dinner, you're just in time." And he seized Coquerico and carried him into the kitchen.

Here the cook popped him into a pot of water and left him, and with the boy went out of the kitchen to attend to something else.

The water began to get warm and then hot. "Oh, Madame Water," cried Coquerico, becoming all at once as meek as a dove, "good and gentle water, best and purest in the world, do not scald me, I beg of you."

"Did you show any pity, selfish wretch?" answered the Water, boiling with indignation. Coquerico leaped out of the pot, knocking off the cover, only to land on the fire.

"Oh, Fire, Fire, do not burn me," he cried, dancing around on his back; "oh, beautiful and brilliant flame, brother of the sun, and cousin of the shining diamond, do not roast me."

"Did you have any pity, you selfish wretch?" cried the Fire, blazing so fiercely with anger that the chick in frightful pain leaped out of a window near by.

But as he landed on the flagging the Wind caught him and whirled him up. "Oh, Wind," shrieked Coquerico, faintly, "oh, kindly Wind, oh, cooling breeze, you make me so dizzy my head reels. Pray let me down that I may rest."

"Let you rest," roared the Wind, "wait and I'll teach you, you selfish wretch."

And with one blast it sent him up so high that as he fell down he stuck on a steeple.

There, if you look, you may see him to this very day, forced at last to help others in this world, a weathervane.

—SPANISH FOLK TALE

THE SCARECROW

Once upon a time there was an old black crow, as old as the hills. And once there was a scarecrow, brand new to his business. The scarecrow was made of a corn stalk wearing the farmer's cast-off hat and coat.

The very first day he took up his post in the cornfield, the old black crow, flying over, laughed at his disguise.

> "Caw, caw, caw," she cried,
>
> "I know you, poor old stalk,
>
> Bloodless is your body,
>
> You neither run nor walk."

The scarecrow kept his temper and said nothing, and this looks as if he were clever. For the old crow had to take herself off without knowing what he was thinking of.

Now the scarecrow *was* clever. He made friends with Magic Darkness and Moving Wind. He had made up his mind to frighten thieving crows away, no matter how old and knowing they might be. And that very evening when the old black crow, as old as the hills, came flying toward the cornfield, with her five black children after her, he whispered, "Now, Magic Darkness and Moving Wind, help me."

And they did. Magic Darkness came down and hid his headlessness, and Moving Wind bent his body and pushed his arms together so that he looked exactly as if he were the farmer stooping to load a gun.

When the old black crow saw this, she whispered, "Turn back, children, and don't speak for your lives;" and although she was as old as the hills, she turned tail as fast as she could, with her five black children after her. When she reached her nest built of sticks in the fork of an apple-tree a quarter of a mile away, she breathed more freely.

"Oh, my children," she panted, "it was no cornstalk scarecrow at all; it was the farmer himself, alive and loading his gun for us."

But when she awoke in the morning light, she felt rather puzzled. "I've seen a good many scarecrows in my time," she said; "I should know a man from a shadow. I'll go and have a look at him in broad daylight."

So as soon as breakfast was over and the crow children had gone to school to hear how featherless children make crow's nests with their fingers, she spread her wings for the cornfield where she had seen the brand new scarecrow. There he stood as plain a humbug as ever deceived the eyes of a blind crow.

"I'm not old enough to be blind yet," she said; "you're a dried-up cornstalk if ever there was one. You'll not frighten me this evening and send me and my children scurrying home." And she sang mockingly,

"Caw, caw, caw,

I know you, poor old stalk,

Bloodless is your body,

You neither run nor walk."

But the clever scarecrow kept his temper and answered never a word. So again the old crow had to take herself off no wiser about his thoughts.

Well, toward evening along came flying again the old black crow, as old as the hills, with her five black children after her. And again the scarecrow whispered, "Now, Magic Darkness and Moving Wind, help me." And they did. Magic Darkness came down and hid his headlessness, and Moving Wind bent his body and pushed his arms together, then straightened him suddenly, like this, halfway, and held his arms out in front, one hand beyond the other, so, as if he were searching for the trigger of a gun.

When the old crow saw him she cried, "Turn back, children, at once," turning herself so suddenly that she bumped into the beak of the first little crow behind her. It was not until she reached her nest built of sticks in the fork of the apple-tree a quarter of a mile away, and had rested a minute, that she breathed freely.

"Oh, my children," she said, "without doubt it was no scarecrow; it was the farmer, alive, and placing his finger on the trigger of his gun to shoot us."

But again when she awoke in the morning light she felt puzzled. "It's very strange," she said. "I've seen a good many scarecrows in my time. I should know a man from a shadow. I'll have another look at him in the broad daylight."

So, as soon as breakfast was over and the crow children had gone to school to hear how featherless grown-ups get crow's feet on their faces, she spread her wings for the cornfield. There stood the scarecrow as plain a humbug as ever deceived the eyes of a blind crow.

"Well," she said, "unless blindness is catching and the bats gave it to me, you're a dried-up corn stalk if ever there was one. If an old crow that was living before you were even thought of knows anything, you'll not frighten me this evening!" And she sang mockingly,

"Caw, caw, caw,

I know you, poor old stalk,

Bloodless is your body,

You neither run nor walk."

But the clever scarecrow kept his temper, and answered never a word. So again the old crow had to take herself off no wiser about his thoughts.

Well, all good things go in threes, as every child who knows more than a crow can tell you. So the third evening along came flying the old black crow, as old as the hills, with her five black children after her. And the third time he whispered, "Now, Magic Darkness and Moving Wind, help me." And the third time they did. Magic Darkness came down and hid his headlessness, and Moving Wind bent him sharply down, lifted him halfway with his arms held out, one hand beyond the other, like this; then suddenly straightened him up with arms pointing up at the crows.

"Don't shoot, dear farmer," shrieked the old crow. She hadn't time to turn tail. "My children and I will let your corn alone until you have harvested it."

Immediately Moving Wind dropped the scarecrow's armless sleeves and brought his hat back to its position on the top of the stalk. And away flew the old crow, as old as the hills, with her five black children after her. When she reached her nest built of sticks in the fork of the apple-tree a quarter of a mile away, and she had rested two minutes, she said, "My children, keep away from that field until I tell you the corn has been gathered in."

When the corn was harvested, the old black crow and her five black children went gleaning to pick up the kernels that had dropped, and fat eating they had. And the scarecrow let them enjoy their meal in peace; his duty was done.

—ANGELA M. KEYES

OEYVIND AND MARIT

There was once a boy named Oeyvind who lived in a hut at the foot of a steep rocky hill. On the roof of the hut walked a little goat. It was Oeyvind's own. Oeyvind kept it there so that it should not go astray, and he carried up leaves and grass to it.

But one fine day the goat leaped down, and away it went up the hill until it came where it never had been before. When Oeyvind ran out of the hut after dinner, he missed his little goat and at once thought of the fox. He looked all about, calling, "Killy-killy-killy-goat!"

"Bay-ay-ay," said the goat, from the top of the hill, as it cocked its head on one side and looked down. And at the side of the goat kneeled a little girl.

"Is it yours, this goat?" she asked.

Oeyvind stared at her, with eyes and mouth wide open, and asked, "Who are you?"

"I am Marit, mother's little one, father's fiddle, grandfather's elf, four years old in the autumn, two days after the frost nights."

"Are you, though?" he said, as soon as he could get his breath.

"Is it yours, this goat?" she asked.

"Yes," he said.

"I should like it. You will not give it to me?"

"No, that I won't."

Marit lay down, kicking her legs and looking up at him, and then she said, "Not if I give you a butter cake for him?"

Oeyvind had eaten butter cake only once in his life, when his grandfather came to visit; anything like it he had never eaten before nor since. "Let me see the butter cake first," said he.

It didn't take Marit long to pull out a large cake. "Here it is," she said, and threw it down to him.

"Ow, it went to pieces," said the boy. He gathered up every crumb, and he couldn't help tasting a very small one. That was so good he had to eat another. Before he knew it he had eaten up the whole cake.

"Now the goat is mine," said the girl, and she laughed and clapped her hands. The boy stopped with the last bit in his mouth.

"Wait a little while?" he begged, for he loved his little goat.

The small girl got up quickly. "No, the goat is mine," she said, and she threw her arms around its neck. She loosened one of her garters and fastened it round the goat's neck and began pulling the goat after her. The goat would not follow: it stretched its neck down to see Oeyvind. "Bay-ay-ay," it said. But the girl took hold of its fleece with one hand and pulled the string with the other, and said, sweetly, "Come, little goat, you shall go into my room and eat out of my apron." And then she sang,

"Come, boy's goat,

Come, mother's calf,

Come, mewing cat

In snow-white shoes;

Come, yellow ducks,

Come out of your hiding-place;

Come little chickens,

Who can hardly go;

Come, my doves

With soft feathers;

See, the grass is wet,

But the sun does you good:

And early, early, is it in summer,

But call for the autumn, and it will come."

And away she went with the goat, calling on all living things she loved to follow her.

The boy stood still as a stone. He had taken care of the goat since the winter before, and he had never thought he would lose it. But now it was gone in a moment and he would never see it again. He lay down and wept.

His mother came along and saw him crying. "What are you crying about?" she asked.

"Oh, the goat, the goat!"

"Yes, where is the goat?" asked the mother, looking up at the roof.

"It will never come back," said the boy.

"Why, how could that happen!"

He could not tell her at once.

"Has the fox taken it?"

"No, oh, no."

"Are your wits gone," said his mother; "what has become of the goat?"

"Oh-h-h—I sold it for—for—a cake!"

As soon as he had said it he knew what it was to sell the goat for a cake.

"What can the little goat think of you, to sell him for a cake?" said his mother.

The boy was so sorry that he said to himself he would never again do anything wrong. He would never cut the thread on the spinning-wheel, he would never let the goats out of the fold, he would never go down to the sea alone. He fell asleep where he lay, and he dreamed that the little goat had gone to heaven and that he sat alone on the roof and could not go to it.

Suddenly there came something wet close up to his ear. He started up. "Bay-ay-ay!" it said. It was the little goat come back.

"What, have you come back?" he cried. He jumped up, took it by the forelegs, and danced with it as if it were a brother. He tickled it and pulled its beard, and set off with it to the hut to tell his mother the good news.

Just then he heard someone behind him; it was the little girl.

"Oh, so it was you brought it back?" said he.

"Grandfather would not let me keep it," said she; "he is waiting near for me."

A sharp voice called out, "Now!" It was her grandfather's, and she remembered what she was to do. She put one of her muddy hands into Oeyvind's and said, "I beg your pardon for taking the little goat." Then she could keep in no longer; she threw her arms around the goat's neck and wept aloud.

"You may have the goat," said Oeyvind.

"Make haste," cried grandfather. So Marit had to go, and Oeyvind had his little goat again.

—BJÖRNSTJERNE BJÖRNSON

BLUNDER

Blunder was going to the Wishing-Gate, to wish for a pair of Shetland Ponies, and a little coach, like Tom Thumb's. And of course you may have your wish, if you once get there. But the thing is, to find it; for it is not, as you imagine, a great gate, with a tall marble pillar on each side, and a sign over the top, like this, WISHING-GATE,—but just an old stile, made of three sticks. Put up two fingers, cross them on the top with another finger, and you have it exactly,—the way it looks, I mean,—a worm-eaten stile, in a meadow; and as there are plenty of old stiles in meadows, how are you to know which is the one?

Blunder's fairy godmother knew, but then she could not tell him, for that was not according to fairy rules and regulations. She could only direct him to follow the road, and ask the way of the first owl he met; and over and over she charged him, for Blunder was a very careless little boy, and seldom found anything, "Be sure you don't miss him,—be sure you don't pass him by." And so far Blunder had come on very well, for the road was straight; but at the turn it forked. Should he go through the wood or turn to the right? There was an owl nodding in a tall oak-tree, the first owl Blunder had seen; but he was a little afraid to wake him up, for Blunder's fairy godmother had told him that this was a great philosopher, who sat up all night to study the habits of frogs and mice, and knew everything but what went on in the daylight, under his nose; and he could think of nothing better to say to this great philosopher than, "Good Mr. Owl, will you please show me the way to the Wishing-Gate?"

"Eh! what's that?" cried the owl, starting out of his nap. "Have you brought me a frog?"

"No," said Blunder, "I did not know that you would like one. Can you tell me the way to Wishing-Gate?"

"Wishing-Gate! Wishing-Gate!" hooted the owl, very angry. "Winks and naps! how dare you disturb me for such a thing as that? Do you take me for a mile-stone? Follow your nose, sir, follow your nose!"—and, ruffling up his feathers, the owl was asleep again in a moment.

But how could Blunder follow his nose? His nose would turn to the right, or take him through the woods, whichever way his legs went, and "what was the use of asking the owl," thought Blunder, "if this was all?" While he hesitated, a chipmunk came scurrying down the path, and, seeing Blunder, stopped short with a little squeak.

"Good Mrs. Chipmunk," said Blunder, "can you tell me the way to the Wishing-Gate?"

"I can't, indeed," answered the chipmunk, politely. "What with getting in nuts, and the care of a young family, I have so little time to visit anything! But if you will follow the brook, you will find an old water-sprite under a slanting stone, over which the water pours all day with a noise like wabble! wabble! who, I have no doubt, can tell you all about it."

So Blunder went on up the brook, and, seeing nothing of the water-sprite, or the slanting-stone, was just saying to himself, "I am sure I don't know where he is,—I can't find it," when he spied a frog sitting on a wet stone.

"Mr. Frog," asked Blunder, "can you tell me the way to the Wishing-Gate?"

"I cannot," said the frog. "I am very sorry, but the fact is, I am an artist. Young as I am, my voice is already remarked at our concerts, and I devote myself so entirely to my profession of music that I have no time for general information. But in a pine-tree beyond, you will find an old crow, who, I am quite sure, can show you the way, as he is a traveler, and a bird of an inquiring turn of mind."

"I don't know where the pine is,—I am sure I can never find him," answered Blunder, discontentedly; but still he went on up the brook, till, hot and tired, and out of patience at seeing neither crow nor pine, he sat down under a great tree to rest. There he heard tiny voices squabbling. And looking about him, Blunder spied a bee, quarreling with a morning-glory elf, who was shutting up the morning-glory in his face.

"Elf, do you know which is the way to the Wishing-Gate?" asked Blunder.

"No," said the elf, "I don't know anything about geography. I was always too delicate to study. But if you will keep on in this path, you will find a Dream-man, coming down from fairyland, with his bags of dreams on his shoulder; and if anybody can tell you about the Wishing-Gate, he can."

"But how can I find him?" asked Blunder, more and more impatient.

"I don't know, I am sure," answered the elf, "unless you look for him."

So there was no help for it but to go on; and presently Blunder passed the Dream-man, asleep under a witch-hazel, with his bags of good and bad dreams laid over him to keep him from fluttering away. But Blunder had a habit of not using his eyes, for at home, when told to find anything, he always said, "I don't know where it is," or, "I can't find it," and then his mother or sister went straight and found it for him. So he passed the Dream-man without seeing him, and went on till he stumbled on Jack-o'-Lantern.

"Can you show me the way to the Wishing-Gate?" said Blunder.

"Certainly, with pleasure," answered Jack, and, catching up his lantern, set out at once.

Blunder followed close, but, in watching the lantern, he forgot to look to his feet, and fell into a hole filled with black mud.

"I say! the Wishing-Gate is not down there," called out Jack, whisking off among the tree-tops.

"But I can't come up there," whimpered Blunder.

"That is not my fault, then," answered Jack, merrily, dancing out of sight.

Oh, a very angry little boy was Blunder, when he clambered out of the hole. "I don't know where it is," he said, crying; "I can't find it, and I'll go straight home."

Just then he stepped on an old, moss-grown, rotten stump; and it happening, unluckily, that this rotten stump was a wood-goblin's chimney, Blunder fell through, headlong, in among the pots and pans in which the goblin's cook was cooking the goblin's supper. The old goblin, who was asleep upstairs, started up in a fright at the tremendous clash and clatter, and, finding that his house was tumbling about his ears, as he thought at first, stumped down to the kitchen to see what was the matter. The cook heard him coming, and looked about her in a fright to hide Blunder.

"Quick!" cried she. "If my master catches you, he will have you in a pie. In the next room stands a pair of shoes. Jump into them, and they will take you up the chimney."

Off flew Blunder, burst open the door, and tore frantically about the room, in one corner of which stood the shoes; but of course he could not see them, because he was not in the habit of using his eyes. "I can't find them! Oh, I can't find them!" sobbed poor little Blunder, running back to the cook.

"Run into the closet," said the cook.

Blunder made a dash at the window, but—"I don't know where it is," he called out.

Clump! clump! That was the goblin, halfway down the stairs.

"Mercy me!" exclaimed cook. "He is coming. The boy will be eaten in spite of me. Jump into the meal-chest."

"I don't see it," squeaked Blunder, rushing towards the fireplace. "Where is it?"

Clump! clump! That was the goblin at the foot of the stairs, and coming towards the kitchen door.

"There is an invisible cloak hanging on that peg. Get into that," cried cook, quite beside herself.

But Blunder could no more see the cloak than he could see the shoes, the closet, and the meal-chest; and no doubt the goblin, whose hand was on the latch, would have found him prancing around the kitchen, and crying out, "I can't find it," but, fortunately for himself, Blunder caught his foot in the invisible cloak, and tumbled down, pulling the cloak over him. There he lay, hardly daring to breathe.

"What was all that noise about?" asked the goblin gruffly, coming into the kitchen.

But as he could see nothing amiss, he went grumbling upstairs again, while the shoes took Blunder up chimney, and landed him in a meadow, safe enough, but so miserable! He was cross, he was disappointed, he was hungry. It was dark, he did not know the way home, and, seeing an old stile, he climbed up, and sat down on the top of it, for he was too tired to stir. Just then came along the South Wind, with his pockets crammed full of showers, and, as he happened to be going Blunder's way, he took Blunder home. The boy was glad enough of this, only he would have liked it better if the Wind had not laughed all the way. For what would you think, if you were walking along a road with a fat old gentleman, who went chuckling to himself, and slapping his knees, and poking himself, till he was purple in the face, when he would burst out in a great windy roar of laughter every other minute?

"What are you laughing at?" asked Blunder, at last.

"At two things that I saw in my travels," answered the Wind; "a hen, that died of starvation, sitting on an empty peck-measure in front of a bushel of grain; and a little boy who sat on the top of the Wishing-Gate, and came home because he could not find it."

"What? what's that?" cried Blunder; but just then he found himself at home. There sat his godmother by the fire, her mouse-skin cloak hung up on a peg, and toeing off a spider's silk stocking an eighth of an inch long; and though everybody cried, "What luck?" and, "Where is the Wishing-Gate?" she sat mum.

"I don't know where it is," answered Blunder. "I couldn't find it;" and thereon told the story of his troubles.

"Poor boy!" said his mother, kissing him, while his sister ran to bring him some bread and milk.

"Yes, that is all very fine," cried his godmother, pulling out her needles, and rolling up her ball of silk; "but now hear my story. There was once a little boy who must needs go to the Wishing-Gate, and his godmother showed him the road as far as the turn, and told him to ask the first owl he met what to do then; but this little boy seldom used his eyes, so he passed the first owl, and waked up the wrong owl; so he passed the water-sprite, and found only a frog; so he sat down under the pine-tree, and never saw the crow; so he passed the Dream-man, and ran after Jack-o'-Lantern; so he tumbled into the goblin's chimney, and couldn't find the shoes and the closet and the chest and the cloak; and so he sat on the top of the Wishing-Gate till the South Wind brought him home, and never knew it. Ugh! Bah!" And away went the fairy godmother up the chimney in such deep disgust that she did not even stop for her mouse-skin cloak.

—Louise E. Chollet

THE GOLDEN PEARS

There was once a poor peasant of Bürs who had nothing in the world but three sons, and a pear-tree that grew in front of his cottage. But the pears were very fine, and the Kaiser was fond of the fruit, so he said to his sons, one day, that he would send the Kaiser a basket as a present. "Perhaps," said he, "if the fruit please him he may help me and mine."

He plaited a krattle, or basket, and lined it with fresh leaves. Then he gathered the finest pears from the tree, large ones as yellow as gold, and laid them on the green leaves.

"Take these to the Kaiser," said he to his eldest son, "and see that thou dost not let anyone rob thee of them by the way."

"Leave that to me, father," said the boy, "I know how to take care of my own. It isn't much anyone will get out of me by asking. I'll have my answer, I can tell you." So he closed up the mouth of the basket with fresh leaves and set out to take the pears to the Kaiser.

It was autumn and the sun struck hot all through the midday hours; so when the boy came at last to a wayside fountain he stopped to drink and to rest in its coolness. A little doubled-up old woman was washing some rags at the fountain and singing a ditty all out of tune. "A witch, I'll be bound," said the boy to himself, "she'll be trying to get my pears, by hook or by crook, but I'll be up to her."

"A fair day, my lad," said the little old wife; "that's a weighty burden you have to carry. What may it be with which you are so heavily laden?"

"A load of sweepings from the road, to see whether I may turn a penny by it," answered the boy, shortly, to stop any further questioning.

"Road-sweepings," repeated the hag, as if she did not believe it. "Belike you don't mean that?"

"But I *do* mean it," retorted the boy.

"Oh, very well. You will find out when you get to your journey's end." And she went on washing and singing her ditty that was all out of tune.

"She means something," said the boy to himself, "that's clear. But at all events my basket is safe. I haven't even let her look at the fruit with her evil eye, so there's no harm done." But he felt uneasy, and as he could not rest, he got up and went on his way.

Soon he reached the palace, and on telling his errand was admitted.

"You have brought me some pears, have you, my boy?" said the Kaiser, well pleased; and his mouth began to water for the luscious fruit.

"Yes, your Majesty, some of the finest golden pears in your Majesty's whole empire," said the boy.

The Kaiser was delighted to hear this and he himself removed the covering of leaves. But what was his anger to find under it nothing but ill-smelling sweepings from the road! The attendants, who stood by, were equally indignant at the insult offered to the emperor, and barely waited for his order to hustle the boy off to prison.

"It is all due to that old hag by the fountain," said he to himself; "I thought she meant mischief to me." This was what he said the first day and the second, but the quiet and solitude of the prison led him to think more closely and to remember the answer he had made to the old wife's question.

"I have often heard my father say," he thought, "how strong truth makes the tongue. Alas, that I did not use it as a weapon to take care of my own."

Meantime the father said to his two sons, "You see how well your elder brother has fared. He kept his eyes wide awake and carried the krattle of golden fruit in safety to the Kaiser, who was no doubt so well pleased with it that he has kept the boy near his person and made him a rich man."

"I am as clever as he," said the second brother; "give me a krattle of the pears and let me take them to the Kaiser, and become a rich man too, only I won't keep it all for myself. I will send for you to share it with me."

"Well said, my son," answered the father; "I have worked hard for you all my life, and it is but meet that in my old age you should share your good fortune with me." And as the season for pears had just come around again, he plaited another krattle and lined it with fresh green leaves and laid in it a goodly heap of the golden fruit.

The second son took the basket and went his way, even in better spirits than his elder brother, for he had the supposed success of the first to give wings to his feet. The autumn sun was as hot through the midday as it had been the year before, so that when he had traveled three days and arrived at the wayside fountain, he too stopped to drink and rest in its coolness. The doubled-up old woman was washing her rags at the fountain and singing her ditty all out of tune. She stopped her croaking as before, to ask him the same question as she had asked his brother.

"It's pigs' wash," said he; "I am taking it to see whether I may turn a penny by it."

"Pigs' wash," repeated she, as if she did not believe it. "Belike you don't mean that?"

"But I do mean it," retorted he, rudely.

And at this she made the same remark she had made his brother.

Sure enough, when the Kaiser removed the leaves, instead of golden pears there was a mess of pigs' wash. The attendants hurried the second boy off to the cell next his brother, and pitched him in with even less ceremony.

Meantime the year was passing away and bringing no tidings to the father of the good fortune promised him by his son. "The ingratitude of children is like a sharp sting," said he, in the bitterness of his grief and disappointment. He would often say to his third son, who was considered too stupid to be good for much, "What a pity it is that you are so dull-headed! If I only dared trust you I might send you to see what has befallen your brothers."

The lad was used to hear himself called a good-for-nothing, so he did not think for a long time that he might even attempt the task. But as the days went by and his father's distress grew more sore, his loving heart was moved, and one day he summoned courage to ask whether he might not try to find his brothers.

"Do you really think you can keep yourself out of harm's way?" exclaimed the father, glad to find the boy anxious to undertake the venture.

"I will do whatever you tell me," said the lad, eagerly.

"Well, you sha'n't go empty-handed, at all events," said the father. And as the pears were just ripe again he laid the choicest of the year's stock in a krattle and sent him on his way.

The boy walked along, looking neither to right nor left, but with his heart beating, lest he should come across the "Harm" out of whose way he had promised to keep himself. All went well, however, except that the sun shone down on him fiercely, so that when he too reached the wayside fountain he was glad to stop to drink and rest in the coolness.

The old wife was washing her rags in the water, and as she patted the linen, singing a ditty all out of tune. "Here comes a third of those surly dogs, I declare," she said to herself, as she saw him arrive with another load of the magnificent pears. "I suppose he'll try to make game of me too as if I didn't know the sweet smell of ripe golden pears from road-sweepings or pigs' wash! a likely thing! But I'm ready for him."

"Good morning, little mother!" said the boy in his direct way, doffing his cap as he had been taught, although she was old and ugly.

"He's sweeter behaved than the other louts, for all he doesn't look so bright-faced," said the hag to herself; and she stopped her song out of tune to return his greeting.

"May I sit down here a bit, please, good mother?" asked the boy, for he was so simple that he thought the fountain must belong to her.

"That you may, and take a draught of the cool water, too," she answered, wondrously softened by his civil manners.

"And what may it be with which you are so laden, my pretty boy?" she asked. "It should be a precious burden to be worth carrying so far as you appear to have come. What have you in your krattle?"

"Precious indeed they are, I believe you," said the boy, "at least so you would think from the store my father sets by them. They are truly golden pears, and he says there are no finer grown in the whole kingdom. I am taking them to the Kaiser, who is fond of the fruit."

"Only ripe pears and yet so heavy," returned the old wife; "one would say it is something heavier than pears. But you'll see when you come to your journey's end."

The boy assured her they were nothing but pears; and as one of his father's commands had been not to lose time by the way, he bade the old dame a courteous farewell and continued on his way.

When the servants saw another peasant boy from Bürs come to the palace with the story that he had pears for the king, they said, "No, no! we've had enough of that! You may turn around and go back." But the poor boy was so disappointed that he could not carry out his task that he sank down on the step and sobbed bitterly, and there he remained sobbing till the Kaiser came out.

The Kaiser's little daughter was with her father. When she saw the boy sobbing, she asked what ailed him, and learned it was another boy from Bürs come to insult the Kaiser with a basket of refuse. And the servants asked her whether they should not take the boy off to prison straightway. The Kaiser left the question to his daughter.

"But I *have* pears," sobbed the boy; "and my father says there are no finer in the empire."

"Yes, yes," jeered the servants, "we know that by heart;" and they attempted to drag him away.

"But won't you look at my pears first, fair princess? The pears that I have brought all this way for the Kaiser? My father will be so sorry."

The princess was struck with the earnestness with which he spoke, and decided to see the basket herself. The moment she said so the boy walked straight up to her with his krattle, so strong in the truth that he felt no fear of the whole troop of lackeys.

The princess removed the leaves and—there indeed were golden pears, not merely yellow with ripeness, but really gold, each, large as it was, a shining pear of solid gold!

"These *are* pears fit for a king," she said, and presented them to her father. The Kaiser was greatly pleased. He ordered the gold fruit to be placed in his cabinet of treasures, and to the boy, as a reward, he promised whatever he should ask.

"All I wish is to find my two brothers, who hold some high office in your Majesty's court," said the boy.

"If those who came with pears before are your brothers, as I suspect, they hold office in prison," said the Kaiser, and commanded that they be brought. As soon as the two were led in, the third ran to them and embraced them. Then the Kaiser bade each tell his story.

"Strong indeed does truth make the tongue to keep its own," said the Kaiser, using almost the same words the boys had often heard their father speak. And they were truly sorry they had not kept his counsel.

The Kaiser sent for the father and gave him and his sons charge of the king's gardens. The father brought with him the pear-tree that, by the power of the truth told of it, had made golden fortune for them. And he and his sons had plenty ever after and were well content.

—Folk Tale

SOME VERY SHORT STORIES

For all little children who fain would tell

What in their tender hearts doth dwell

THE PUPPY'S BARK

Our puppy is so little that he can hardly stand up. But he wants the kitten to think him a big dog. So the other day he steadied himself on his legs and tried to give a loud bark. "Bow wow," he said. And down he tumbled.

WHAT HAPPENED TO THE WHITE KITTEN

Once when a white kitten spied the tip of her tail, she tried to catch it. Round and round she went so fast that she turned into a white ball. But, of course, the tail went as fast as she did, so she couldn't catch up with it. Soon she grew so dizzy that she had to stop. There she was back again, a sensible white kitten.

A CONCEITED GRASSHOPPER

The other day a very young grasshopper and an old rooster were out in the field together.

"I can jump higher than anyone in this field," cried the grasshopper. The rooster said nothing, but opened his mouth as if he meant to yawn.

"Here I go," cried the grasshopper, and she jumped so high that she landed in the rooster's mouth. The rooster gobbled her up.

And that was the end of her and her boasting.

THE MOUSE'S ESCAPE

A little gray mouse lived in a hole in our kitchen closet. One day she smelled some cheese. "M-m," she said, "how delicious!" She peeped out to see whether Tom, our cat, was in the kitchen. He wasn't. Out she stole, sniffed about, and found the cheese. Just as she began to nibble it, along came Tom. The little mouse darted back into her safe hole.

WHAT THE WHITE HEN DID FOR THE WORLD

One morning the white hen went into the barn. The rooster saw her go, but he didn't stop her. After a few minutes out she came, clucking to the whole world, "Cut-cut-cut-cut-cadah-cut! Cut-cut-cut-cut-cadah-cut!" And the whole world as well as the rooster knew she had laid an egg.

THE GOLDEN GOOSE

Once a man owned a wonderful goose. Every morning when he said, "Lay," it laid a golden egg. By and by the man grew so greedy that he wanted all the golden eggs at once. So he cut open the goose. There wasn't one egg in it. And, of course, the goose couldn't lay any more eggs now. The foolish man had killed the goose that laid the golden eggs.

—ÆSOP

THE MOON AND HER MOTHER

(This story may be accompanied by blackboard sketches of the phases of the moon.)

One day the moon asked her mother for a cloak that would fit her well.

"How can I make a cloak that will fit you?" answered the mother. "You are always changing your size. One day you are a new moon. Another day you are a full moon. And another day you are neither."

So the little moon has to go without a cloak.

—Old Fable

MOTHER CAREY'S CHICKENS

One day in winter the snowflakes came down as soft and light and white as feathers. The little children looking out at the window sang,

"Old Mother Carey's chickens,

Old Mother Carey's chickens;

They are up in the sky,

Ever so high;

Old Mother Carey's chickens."

Down fell the snowflakes, thick and fast, and more and more and more, till they made a snowstorm.

When they were all down the children brought out their sleds, and away they went coasting on Mother Carey's chickens' feathers.

THE STORY OF THE WEE, WEE BONE

Once a wee, wee girl came across a wee, wee dog scratching a wee, wee hole to bury a wee, wee bone. When the wee, wee dog had buried the wee, wee bone, he trotted off on his wee, wee legs. And when he had gone a wee, wee way, the wee, wee girl dug her wee, wee fingers into the wee, wee hole, and took away the wee, wee bone.

But the wee, wee dog smelled her out with his wee, wee nose and said, "Give me back my wee, wee bone; you can't eat it and I can." The wee, wee girl wouldn't.

Then the wee, wee dog sat up on his wee, wee hind legs and cried a wee, wee tear. This made the wee, wee girl sorry. So she gave the wee, wee dog his wee, wee bone.

The wee, wee dog dried the wee, wee tear with his wee, wee paw, and ate up the wee, wee bone.

And that's the end of this wee, wee story.

THE MISSING LAMB

One evening a shepherd was turning away from the fold when one of the sheep bleated mournfully.

"Is thy lamb missing, poor mother?" asked the shepherd.

Just then he heard a loud bark, and there half a field away was Carlo, his dog, guiding home a frightened lamb. The little creature had strayed away from her mother to find the very sweetest bits of sheep sorrel.

"Bow wow, master," called Carlo, "don't close up yet."

"Ba-a-a, ba-a-a-a," cried the little lamb, "dear mother, where are you?"

The mother heard her and bounded into the air with joy. "Ba-a-a, come to me, my lamb," she called, "come to me, my lambkin, my wee lambkin, my wee wee little lamb."

The little lamb leaped to her mother's side and was safe in the fold.

The shepherd patted Carlo on the head and called him "Good dog" and said, "Come with me, my dog, and I'll give thee a bone thick with meat."

THE ANT AND THE DOVE

Once an ant went to the bank of a river to quench her thirst. As she stooped to the water she fell in and was nearly drowned. A dove perched on a tree overhanging the river saw her and quickly dropped down a leaf to her. The ant climbed up on the leaf and it floated to the bank. She went ashore, safe and sound.

Not long after this, a bird catcher stepped softly up to the tree to set a snare to catch the dove. The ant saw him and quickly stung him in the foot. The bird catcher's cry at the pain startled the dove. Away she flew, safe and sound.

—ÆSOP

THE BOY AND THE NUTS

A boy put his hand into a jar to take some nuts. He grasped so many that there was no room for his hand to come out. In a great fright he burst into tears.

"Be satisfied with half as many," said a man who was watching him, "and your hand will come out easily."

The greedy boy dropped half, and at once out came his hand.

—ÆSOP

DID SHE CATCH HIM?

One day a little girl said to her wisest aunt, "I wish I could catch that sparrow."

"The next time he comes," said her wisest aunt, "shake some salt on his tail. But be sure not to let him see nor hear you."

The little girl went into the house and brought out some salt. Pretty soon the sparrow alighted near her. She tiptoed up behind him with the salt ready in her hand. Nearer and nearer she stole.

Just as she stooped to shake the salt on his tail, the sparrow cocked his head at her and flew away.

THE BEARS AT PLAY

A small brown bear and a small black bear walked up to each other and rubbed noses.

"Will you play with me if I play with you?" whispered the brown one to the other. And the other whispered, "I will."

The two trotted out to the center of the cage. The brown one turned a somersault and the black one turned a bigger somersault. After this they both turned somersaults together.

When the play was over, they rubbed noses again and each went back to his own cave in the rocks.

HOW THE GROCER PLAYED A TRICK ON KIT

Kit was the grocer's horse. One day as the grocer came up to her she whinnied and rubbed her nose against his pocket.

"Ha, ha, ha, I've caught you this time; it isn't in my pocket," said the grocer; "here it is." He held out to her a ripe red apple he had been hiding behind his back.

Kit didn't wait to laugh at the joke; she ate the apple in one big bite.

THE SHORT TALE OF THE RABBITS WHO WENT OUT TO SEE THE WORLD

Two white rabbits lived in a hutch in our back yard. One sunny morning said One to the Other, "Let us go out to see the world."

So they did. They went up the alley way to the front garden. Here the grass was growing fresh and green.

"Ah," said the Other to One, "the world was made for us. It is nothing but a big cabbage leaf. Taste it."

Just as they put their noses down to nibble a bit of it, a dog poked *his* nose through the railing and said, "Bow wow."

"Oh my, the world belongs to him," they cried; "he may have it."

And back they scurried to their safe hutch.

There they stayed, eating cabbage leaves and letting the world alone.

THE DISPUTE BETWEEN THE POT AND THE KETTLE

The pot said the kettle was black. And the kettle said the pot was black. And the pot said the kettle was black. And the kettle said the pot was black. And they kept it up.

In the middle of the dispute in came two servants. One seized the pot and the other seized the kettle, and they scrubbed them both within an inch of their lives. So I suppose the servants thought both were black. What do you think?

HOW THE TURTLE GOT HIS DINNER

It was the small black turtle's dinner time. He drew in his head and watched. A bluebottle buzzed by, singing. Snap! out came the turtle's head. The bluebottle's song was over, the turtle was eating him for dinner.

"A bluebottle is a delicious morsel," said the turtle aloud to anyone who might happen to be passing.

He dined that day on foolish bluebottles who didn't know he had a head.

THE CATERPILLAR CAUGHT IN THE RAIN

The other day a caterpillar was out walking on a leaf, when it began to rain. He had no umbrella, but that did not bother him. He crawled under the leaf, and waited for the shower to be over.

When the rain-drops stopped pattering over his head, he stuck out his head to see whether the sky had cleared. It had. A beautiful rainbow was just fading out of the sky.

Up the caterpillar climbed, dry and comfortable, and went on with his walk.

THE SONG THE COCKLE-SHELL SINGS

One day Anna Lucy held a cockle-shell to her ear. She listened and then began to smile.

"Do you hear anything?" asked her little brother Frank.

"Yes," answered Anna Lucy, "you may hear it too." She held the shell to Frank's ear. Frank listened, then he began to smile. "What is it?" he whispered.

"It is the song of the sea," said Anna Lucy; "the shell sings it in her heart."

THE WATER-SNAIL'S RIDE

A little water-snail with his house on his back floated on the top of the water. Suddenly he must have thought of something downstairs that he needed, for he drew himself into his house. Down it went to the bottom of the water. The water-snail stuck out his horns and head, and ate up a tiny bit of seaweed. So I suppose that is what he needed. In he drew himself again, and up went his house just as if it were an elevator.

"You must find that house very convenient," said I to him. But he said nothing to me; he only floated on the top of the water.

IT TAKES TIME TO GROW

A toadstool sprang up in a night. But it fell to earth next day when the first passer-by touched it. An acorn took a hundred years to grow into an oak. But the oak is still standing, strong and tall.

THE FRIGHT THEY HAD

One day as a snail with his house on his back crawled up a vine he met a ladybug. The two stopped to chat about their children. All of a sudden a little girl, who was passing, cried out,

"Ladybug, Ladybug, fly away home,

Your house is on fire,

Your children all burned."

Home flew Ladybug, pale with fright.

"How thankful I am," said the snail, "that I carry my house on my back!" But on second thought he too turned pale with fright. "Perhaps my darling children will crawl near poor Ladybug's house to see the fire, and be burned to death." He turned about and crawled home as fast as his snail's pace would let him, and that wasn't very fast.

But it was all a joke; it happened on April Fool's Day. The snail's children were quite safe and so were Ladybug's.

"Ha, ha, ha, Mr. Snail, you're an April Fool," cried the little girl, skipping past again.

But I don't know whether they understood her. What do you think?

HIMSELF

"Who are you?" said Tom, to a small black shadow beside him.

"Why, I'm you," said the shadow; "don't you know me?"

"What, a little fellow like you!" cried Tom; "you're very much mistaken." And away he strode.

"No, a big fellow like you," said the shadow, as he shot out in front of Tom.

WHY THE CANARY SANG IN HIS CAGE

A canary swung in his golden cage and sang joyously. The window was open, so a lark heard him as she rose into the air. She alighted on the window sill in wonder.

"How can you sing shut up in a cage!" she exclaimed. "Come out into the free air and up into the sky with me."

The canary stopped his song to listen to the lark. "Why do you stop singing, little canary?" asked a sick boy, in a feeble voice. He was in a bed near the canary's cage. The lark could not see him, but she heard him. "Your song," said the boy, "makes me forget my pain."

The canary burst into a sweeter song. "Now I know," said the lark, "he sings because it makes the sick boy happy." And she flew upward, wiser than before.

WHO THE BIRD WAS

One hot day in July a bird perched at the very top of a tall hemlock. The blazing sun shone on his scarlet body and made it glow like fire.

"What a foolish bird to be out in the scorching sun," cried Mother Robin to her husband. "He'll be sunstruck." She and Father Robin stood shading their eyes under the cool maple leaves to look up at him. "Who can he be?"

"I think, my dear," said Father Robin, "that I had better go up and tell him to come down."

"Oh," cried Mother Robin, "what would the birdlings and I do if anything should happen to you!" and she caught him by the tail just as he was flying off.

As Father Robin opened his mouth to answer, the scarlet bird spread shining black wings and flew into the sunshine, singing,

"I love the sun, the light, the flame,

Scarlet tanager is my name."

"Never fear for him," said Mother Robin, "the sun and he are good friends."

HOW THE OLD TROUT SERVED TOM

Once a water-baby named Tom swam close to some little trout. He began tormenting them and trying to catch them. They slipped through his fingers and jumped clean out of the water in their fright.

As Tom chased them he swam near a dark pool under an alder root. Out floushed a huge old brown trout ten times as big as he. She ran straight at Tom and knocked nearly all the breath out of his body.

So it was Tom's turn to be frightened. After that you may be sure he let the little trout alone.

—From KINGSLEY

A CLEVER COW

A quick-witted old cow learned how to shake apples down from the trees. While rubbing herself against the tree she noticed that an apple sometimes fell. She rubbed a little harder, and more apples fell. Soon the farmer had to keep an eye on her to save his apples.

—From BURROUGHS

THE SNOWMAN

When the sun got up one morning in winter he found a snowman staring at him rudely.

"Don't stare at me. If you do you'll melt," said the sun.

"Indeed!" said the snowman. "A cat may look at a king. I'll look at you if I like." And he stared harder than ever.

Pretty soon he felt the top of his head softening. "I feel very queer," said he to himself. But he didn't stop staring. "Ugh!" he shivered, "water is running down my back. My nose is going. My toes are going. I'm going."

And he went.

THE RACE

The kitten lay curled up in a ball fast asleep. The pup was broad awake.

He stole up to kitty, lifted his paw, and gave her a tap on the nose. Then he scampered off. Up started kitty, and round and round the kitchen went the pup with kitty after him.

It made the kitchen clock so dizzy to watch them that she put up her long hand to steady her head.—"One," rang the bell inside of her.

"Time's up," cried the pup. And he and kitty sat down on the mat side by side and the pup put out his tongue and laughed at the fun.

BRAVE DAN

Everybody was out. So of course Dan, the pup, was master of the house. He trotted proudly through the halls and poked his nose into every room, for burglars.

In his master's room he heard something say, "Tick, tick, tick, tick." Dan pricked up his ears. Somebody was in the house. Who could it be? A glove lay on the floor near the mantel. Dan walked over and began to sniff at it.

"One," struck the clock on the mantelpiece. Dan scampered off as fast as his legs could carry him.

THE WIND'S FROLIC

"Down you go," cried the wind to the leaves one morning in autumn. And down he blew them in crowds from the trees, brown ones, red ones, and yellow ones. Then he drove them scurrying before him up the street. At last he swirled them together in heaps, and left off to rest.

So there we too shall let them lie.

THE DEAD CANARY

The little yellow canary that used to sing so sweetly grew sick and died. The children wept to see it.

"Let us bury him under the apple-tree," said Alice; "every spring it will cover his grave with white blossoms."

So Robert dug a small grave under the apple-tree, and Alice laid the canary gently in it. They covered him with the soft earth.

Every spring the apple-tree sent down his white blossoms on the grave.

THE SWAN'S MEAL

One morning as a shining white swan sailed about on the lake he saw a boy on the bank, eating some bread. He swam over to the boy and thrust out his long white neck toward the bread.

"The beautiful swan wants my bread," cried the boy. He was delighted.

He broke it and threw it bit by bit on a lily pad. The swan ate it, to the last crumb. Then he bent his head as if to thank the boy, and sailed away.

THE BOY AND THE FROGS

Some boys at play near a pond began to pelt the frogs with stones, just for the fun of seeing them go under water. They killed several of them.

At last one of the frogs lifted his head high out of the water, and cried out, "Pray stop, boys; what is fun for you is death to us."

"That is true," said one of the boys; "let us leave the poor creatures in peace." And they did.

—From ÆSOP

SWEET PORRIDGE

There was a poor but good little girl who lived alone with her mother. One day they no longer had anything to eat. The child went out into the forest, and there an old woman gave her a wonderful little pot. When you said to it, "Cook, little pot, cook," it would cook good sweet porridge. And when you said, "Stop, little pot, stop," it would stop cooking. The girl took the pot home to her mother, and they were no longer hungry, but ate sweet porridge whenever they chose.

Once when the girl had gone out her mother said, "Cook, little pot, cook." The mother ate till she was satisfied. But when she wanted the pot to stop she found she did not know the word. So it went on cooking and the porridge rose over the edge. STILL it cooked on until the kitchen and the whole house were full, and then the next house, and then the whole street, as if it meant to feed the whole world. No one could stop it.

At last when only one house remained the child came home from the opposite direction and just said, "Stop, little pot, stop," and it stopped.

But whoever wished to come back to the town that night had to eat his way back.

—Folk story

FINDING A HOME

Early in spring a couple of bluebirds set out to look for a home.

"What do you think of this vacant dove-cote for our nest, sweet wife?" asked he. "The view from the top of the gable is beautiful."

"I am afraid of all these windows," said she, peeping in at each. "The wind might prove too strong for our little ones when they come."

"Parents must think of that," said he. And on they flew.

Under the eaves of a barn they found an empty swallow's nest. "The very thing for us," they both cried, and alighted to look at it. At this minute who should arrive from the south but the swallow who owned it? He saw at once what they were at and flew straight into it, crying,

"Kwi-kwi-kwivet,

My house is not to let."

"How delightful to own a home of your own," said the she-bluebird.

"Isn't it?" agreed the he-bluebird.

"Is that a wren's house over there?" asked she, flying over. But when she attempted to poke her nose inside, out rushed two little wrens at her and scolded her away.

"My love," said he, "how you are trembling. Let us build a house of our own."

And that's what they did. In a stump in an open field they found exactly the hole they wanted and there they made their nest.

It wasn't long before their little ones came and found it the snuggest in the world.

DID JIP DINE ON CHICKEN?

One day a dog named Jip went for a walk. He came to a yard where there was a hen with her brood of chicks. Said Jip to himself, "A downy little yellow chick would make a sweet dinner for a dog. I think I'll have it." He turned in at the gate. But Mother Hen had something to say about it. "Cluck, cluck," she cried to her chicks, and spread out her wings to hide them. Then she lowered her head, stuck out her sharp beak, and made straight for Jip. He turned tail and fled home as fast as his legs would carry him.

THE DOG IN THE MANGER

Once when some oxen went to their manger to eat hay they found a small dog in it. The dog growled and snapped at the oxen and would not let them come near the hay. The stableman saw it all. "Get out of there, you selfish cur!" he cried to the dog. "You cannot eat the hay yourself and you will not let those who can." He seized a whip and the dog was glad to run yelping away.

—From ÆSOP

THE TWO APPLES

A real apple and a clay apple lay side by side. The real apple was jealous of the clay apple. A little girl had smoothed and pressed and patted the cheek of the clay apple, but she had only looked at him. Soon along came the little girl with her hat and coat on. She picked up the real apple. "Come, ripe red apple," said she; "we'll go visiting. I know a little lame boy who will like a bite of you. My clay apple would never do for that."

As she looked at him, the real apple felt himself turning a deeper red, he was so ashamed that he had been jealous.

THE DOG AND THE SHADOW

A dog was crossing a stream of water, with a piece of meat in his mouth. As he looked down, he thought he saw another dog with a larger piece of meat. Said the greedy fellow to himself, "I'll have that too." He dropped his own meat and sprang into the water after the shadow. The real meat fell into the water and floated away.

—ÆSOP

THE QUARREL

One morning Tom's right foot said to Tom's left foot, "Let me go first."

"No," said Tom's left foot, "you let me go first."

"No," said Tom's right foot, "you let me go first."

And they began all over again.

Suddenly Tom's left ear remarked to Tom's right ear, "Perhaps, the silly things will set out together."

"The very thing to do," cried both feet, and they started off. This left Tom without a leg to stand on. So he fell down and bruised them both.

They were black and blue for three whole days.

WHAT HAPPENED TO THE WAX DOLL

The wax doll went to visit the rag doll and sat in a sunny window, where the people passing might admire her.

"How handsome you are," said the rag doll. "I wish I had large blue eyes and red and white cheeks. That white silk dress is very becoming."

The wax doll only stared and smiled.

"Towser, the dog, leads me a life of it," went on the rag doll. She felt she must make conversation for her guest. "Why," said she, "the other day he tore me almost to pieces, when—" She stopped suddenly. Something dreadful was happening to the wax doll. Her face was running down on her white silk dress.

Just then in came the little girl who owned the dolls. "Dear, dear me," said she, "the wax doll has melted," and she threw her into a corner.

"After all," said the rag doll to herself, thoughtfully, "I am not beautiful, and Towser troubles me, but I have much to be thankful for."

THE ROUTING OF TOM

One morning Tom met the geese on their way to the pond, and for once the gander was not leading them. Tom made sure of this. Gander had once chased him half a mile for teasing the geese.

"I'll be master instead of the gander," said he to the geese. "Shoo! back you go." He spread out his arms to drive them back. When they turned to go, he ran around in front of them. "Shoo! forward you go," said he. Once more the geese set off hopefully for the pond. "Shoo! back you go," cried Tom. So he kept the poor geese running back and forth distracted.

At last one small goose plucked up her courage. "Hiss-s-s-s," she cried, stretching out her long neck toward Tom. Instantly out went twenty necks and twenty geese made for Tom, crying, "Hiss-ss-ss-ss." Tom took to his heels.

MRS. VIXEN AND HER CUBS AT PLAY

Under a rock lay a great brown, sharp-nosed creature, with a white tip to her brush, and round her four or five little cubs, the funniest fellows you ever saw. It was Mrs. Vixen, a mother fox, and her children.

The mother lay on her back, rolling about, and stretching out her legs and head and tail in the bright sunshine. The cubs jumped over her, and ran around her, and nibbled her paws, and lugged her about by the tail, and she enjoyed it mightily.

But one selfish little fellow put an end to all the fun. He stole away from the rest to a dead crow close by, and dragged it off to hide it, though it was nearly as big as himself. His brothers caught him at it and set off after him in full cry. Before they knew it they were seen by a man. They left the dead crow and ran back to tell their mother.

Up jumped Mrs. Vixen. She caught the smallest one up in her mouth, and the rest toddled after her. Soon she had them safe at home in a dark opening in the rocks. But the fun was over for that day.

—From Kingsley

THE FOOLISH HOOP

"Why do you strike me and hold me in?" cried the hoop to the stick.

"Shall I let you go?" asked the stick.

"Do," said the hoop; "I do not need your guidance."

"Very well," said the stick. And she let him go. Down the street rolled the hoop. Fast and faster he went. He could not stop himself. A turn in the flags headed him straight toward the street. Out he plunged under the wheels of a passing wagon, and was crushed to pieces.

HOW THE CLOCK CAME INTO THE STORY

Once a little round-faced clock lived on the desk of a man who wrote stories. The clock had a chance to hear most of the stories. For when the man finished a story he usually called a beautiful lady into the room and read it to her. The beautiful lady laughed at the fun in the story and the little clock's face shone. But perhaps that is what a clean little clock's face always does.

One day the man read from the story, "The prince and the princess were married just as the clock struck"—"One!" rang the little clock. Its heart almost stopped beating; it had not meant to interrupt the story.

The beautiful lady cried, "Why, the clock knows the story." But she laughed as she said it.

What do you think about it?

BABY GOES ON A VOYAGE

The other day baby went on a voyage on the good ship *Hands and Knees*. She crept out into the hall so softly that mother did not hear her go.

Out there was the cuckoo clock that said "R-r-r-r-." Baby stopped and looked up at it. A door in the clock opened, and out came a little bird who cried, "Cuck-oo, cuck-oo, cuck-oo." In he went again and the door shut.

Baby gurgled with glee. "I tee oo," she cried. She sat down to wait for the little bird to come out and play again.

But mother found her, and carried her back on the good ship *Mother's Arms*.

THE RUNAWAYS

One day four little white pigs and three little white geese met together near Rover's kennel. But they were so full of themselves that they did not notice where they were.

"We stole out while Mother Sow was dozing after dinner," screamed the little pigs. They laughed so much they rolled on the ground.

"We stole out while Mother Goose was gabbling with a neighbor," giggled the little geese. And they hugged their sides to think how clever they were.

"What's this! what's this!" growled Rover, coming to the door of his kennel.

The pigs squealed with fright and the geese clacked in terror. All took to their heels, back to their mothers.

THE NAIL

A merchant had done good business at the fair; he had sold his wares, and filled his bag with gold and silver. Then he set out at once on his journey home, for he wished to be in his own house before night. He packed his bag with the money on his horse, and rode away.

At noon he rested in a town; when he wanted to go on, the stable-boy brought out his horse, and said,—

"A nail is wanting, sir, in the shoe of its left hind foot."

"Let it be wanting," answered the merchant; "the shoe will stay on for the six miles I have still to go. I am in a hurry." In the afternoon, when he once more got down and had his horse fed, the stable-boy went into the room to him, and said,—

"Sir, a shoe is wanting from your horse's left hind foot. Shall I take him to the blacksmith?"

"Let it still be wanting," said the man; "the horse can very well hold out for a couple of miles more. I am in a hurry."

He rode forth, but before long the horse began to limp. It had not limped long before it began to stumble, and it had not stumbled long before it fell down and broke its leg. The merchant had to leave the horse where it was, and unstrap the bag, take it on his back, and go home on foot. And he did not get there until quite late at night.

"That unlucky nail," said he to himself, "has made all this trouble."

Make haste slowly.

—Old Tale

THE SOAP BUBBLES

Anna Mary invited Dan, her dog, into the yard to see her make soap bubbles. She blew out a beautiful one shining with all the colors of the rainbow.

Dan watched it as it floated on the air. "What can the lovely thing be?" thought he to himself. It passed close to him. He put out his paw to touch it. The delicate bubble was gone. There was nothing but a wet spot on Dan's inquisitive nose.

"Goosy Dan," said Anna Mary, scolding him, "lovely moons floating in the air are not to be touched by clumsy paws."

She blew the next one high above Dan's head.

THE PEACOCK'S TAIL

The peacock pretended not to see anyone. He strutted about picking up corn. But he must have glanced out of the corner of his eye every time he stooped for another kernel. For when a crowd had gathered he left off eating and faced about in front of the people.

He swelled out his chest till he could not see his ugly feet. Out he spread slowly his shining blue and green tail with its hundreds of eyes. It came up around his head like a gorgeous frame.

All the little boys and girls in the crowd held their breath until it came out in a great "Ah!" The peacock let them look a whole minute. Then he lowered his tail and strutted away.

HOW THE ROOSTER WAS DECEIVED

The rooster with the reddest comb perched himself up on the gate-post to crow. As he stretched his neck he caught sight of another rooster higher up on the barn.

"I'll have no one in this barnyard higher than I," said he; "I am master here." And he flew up at the rooster. But his wings were so short that he barely reached the edge of the roof. Had he fallen he would have been disgraced before all the fowls in the barnyard. He was so furious at the thought that he rushed up the sloping roof and pecked at the rooster savagely. The rooster never budged.

"Ha, ha, silly cockscomb!" screamed Poll, the parrot, shaking with laughter. "It serves you right. Did you hurt your beak? He isn't a live rooster at all. He's only a weathervane."

THE SHOES THAT WALKED MOST

The cobbler sat at his bench. The shoes stood in a row before him.

"Which shall I mend first?" thought he to himself. "I know," he said aloud; "I'll begin with whichever pair has walked most."

At this out toddled baby's shoes.

The cobbler laughed at them. "Why," said he, "baby has been in the world only two years at most. You can't have walked far yet."

"Well," said the shoe for the right foot, "baby's mother says we never stop going until she takes us off at night. We notice that grown people sit down a great deal."

"Well, well," said the cobbler, "have your way." So he waxed his thread and sewed a patch on each small sole.

WHAT O'CLOCK?

Mary and Anna Jane were playing in the fields. Suddenly Mary stopped and said, "I wonder what time it is. Mother said we should go home at four o'clock."

A dandelion spoke up politely. "My head will tell you what o'clock it is," said he. "Blow it off, and, as you blow, count."

"You are very kind, sir," said Anna Jane. Mary was too much astonished to speak.

Anna Jane blew once. "One o'clock," said she.

"Go on," cried the dandelion. "My head is at your service."

Anna Jane went on blowing and counting. "Two o'clock, three o'clock, four o'clock." The whole head was off.

"Thank you, dandelion," said Anna Jane, although she was not sure whether the dandelion could hear without his head. "It's time for us to be going home."

So Anna Jane and Mary went home at the right time.

THE WONDERFUL CHANGE

It was time for the caterpillar to shut himself in and prepare for a new life. So he chose a low branch and began spinning his cocoon about him. He made it firm and strong, so that no one should break through it and disturb him. It wrapped him about like a shroud. The caterpillar lay down in it and waited.

Days passed and a new day came. The caterpillar burst from the cocoon, changed most gloriously; no longer a crawling worm, but a splendid butterfly with wings. At first he tried his wings timidly. Soon he spread them wide and flew up into the sunshine.

Grown people as well as little children wondered at the change, and felt joy in it.

HOW NAN AND THE MOON WENT FOR A WALK

One evening as Nan started out for a walk the white moon in the sky went before her.

"Why, the moon is coming, too," said Nan, and she stood still, she was so surprised. The white moon stood still too. Nan walked on faster. The white moon went faster before her. At the corner Nan turned to go home. Now the white moon was behind, but it followed her even to the door. Nan looked up at it before going in, and the white moon looked down at Nan.

That night before she jumped into bed Nan looked out of the window. There in the starry sky was the moon gazing down at her.

"Were you waiting for me all this time, moon?" asked Nan. "I can't come out until to-morrow night. We'll have another walk then."

And they did.

WHAT CHRISTOPHER COLUMBUS DID

A great many years ago in far-off Italy lived Christopher Columbus. He did a wonderful thing. He and some companions and sailors set out in three small ships to cross the great wide ocean. The huge waves tossed the ships about and came up over their bows. The sailors were so terrified they begged Columbus to turn back. But he was too brave to do that. He kept on till he came to a new country. It was America, our country. Then he and all with him knelt on the shore and gave thanks to God.

WHAT THE MOON SAW

"Yesterday," said the Moon to me, "I looked down into a small yard. There sat a clucking hen with eleven chicks, and a pretty little girl was running and jumping around them. The poor hen didn't know what to make of it. She screamed and spread out her wings over her brood. The noise brought the girl's father out. He scolded his daughter and sent her into the house. I glided on and thought no more about it.

"But this evening, only a few minutes ago, I looked down into the same yard. The hen and her chicks had gone to roost. Everything was quiet. Out came the little girl, crept to the hen-house, pushed back the bolt, and slipped in. The hen and chicks cried out at once and came fluttering down from their perches. I saw it all, for I looked through a hole in the hen-house wall. I was angry with the obstinate child. And so was her father. He came out and seized her by the arm.

"'What are you about?' he asked.

"The little girl wept and sobbed. 'I wanted to kiss the hen and beg her pardon for frightening her yesterday, but she does not understand."

"'I do now,' said her father. And he kissed her on the forehead and on the mouth and on the eyes. 'You are my own sweet little daughter. The hen will understand best if you let her alone.'"

—HANS CHRISTIAN ANDERSEN

THE ELF WHO STAYED OUT TOO LATE

In a beautiful rose there dwelt a little elf. With a fairy microscope you could see his wings reaching from his shoulders to his feet. Without it you couldn't see him at all.

One day when he went out into the sunshine to play he had such fun that he forgot all about getting home in time. He flew from flower to flower. He danced on the wings of the passing butterfly. Best of all, he measured how many steps it would take to cross all the roads made of veins on the geranium leaf.

It was this that delayed him so long. Before he knew it the sun was down, dewdrops sprinkled the leaf, and the night began to darken. The poor little elf was very much frightened. He began to shiver, too, with the cold. Indeed, he grew so numb that he could hardly spread his wings to fly back to the rosebush. But he managed it.

The beautiful rose was just closing her petals for the night. In he dived under the warm leaves.

THE BOLD WEED

The weed smelled rank to heaven. But she looked out at everyone as bold as brass.

"Hold up your heads," she cried to the violets. "Push yourselves forward where people may see you."

But the violets held down their heads modestly.

Along came Lucy looking for some flowers. "Ugh! what a rank smell that weed has!" she cried. She plucked it up by the root and threw it on a heap of rubbish. But she gathered a great bunch of the dewy violets for her grandmother's birthday.

ODDS AND ENDS

There was once on a time a maiden who was pretty but very lazy and wasteful. When a little knot came in the flax she was spinning, she at once pulled out a whole heap of it and threw it away. Her servant gathered up the bits of flax that had been thrown away, cleaned them, spun them, and wove them into a piece of fine linen. Out of this she made herself a beautiful dress.

Well, the maiden was to be married. On the eve of the wedding the servant was dancing about in the pretty dress she had made. The bride said to the bridegroom, "How that girl jumps about dressed in my odds and ends!" The bridegroom asked the bride what she meant. Then she told him that the servant was wearing a dress made of the flax she had thrown away. When the bridegroom heard that, he knew how lazy and wasteful she was.

"The other girl is the wife for me," said he. And he married the other girl in the very dress she had made out of the odds and ends.

—Folk Tale

ABRAHAM LINCOLN'S KINDNESS

One day as Abraham Lincoln rode along on his horse he saw a pig struggling to keep herself from sinking into a deep place filled with mud. The poor thing was squealing in terror, because the mud was sucking her in.

At first Lincoln rode by without stopping. But his kind heart could not forget the pig. He turned back, got down from his horse, and drew the pig out of the mud.

THE ANT AND THE GRASSHOPPER

There was once a foolish little grasshopper that spent all her time playing. Through the long summer and autumn she did nothing but sing from morning till night. So when winter came and the snow covered the ground, she hadn't a morsel of food stored away in her house.

Soon she was so faint with hunger that she begged her neighbor, the ant, to give her something to eat. "I am starving," she said; "give me a grain of wheat."

"Why did you not save some grain at harvest time?" asked the ant. "There was plenty to be had. What were you doing?"

"I was singing," answered the grasshopper. "I had no time for work."

"Hoity toity!" cried the ant; "if you sang all summer you must dance hungry to bed in winter."

—ÆSOP

THE DONKEY AND THE MULE

A donkey and a mule set out with their master on a long journey. Each animal carried a load.

As he climbed the steep path up a mountain the donkey felt his load heavier than he could bear. He begged the mule to help him. "Help me, brother," he cried, "or I shall drop." But the mule pretended not to hear. After struggling along a little farther the poor donkey fell dead.

The master now placed the donkey's load on the mule, giving him two loads to carry. And on top of both he piled the donkey.

"It serves me right," said the mule to himself; "had I helped the donkey I should not now be carrying his burden."

—ÆSOP

WHY THE MAGPIE'S NEST IS BADLY MADE

Once on a time, when the world was very young, the magpie was the only bird that did not know how to build a nest. She told her trouble to the other birds and they all met to teach her.

"Place that stick there," said the blackbird. He flew over and did it for her himself.

"Oh," said the magpie, "I knew that before."

"Place this stick here," said the thrush, placing it for her.

"Oh," said the magpie, "I knew that before."

The wren and the robin, the goldfinch and the chaffinch, the lark and the swallow, and many other birds went on showing her how to build the nest. As each bit was added, she said, "Oh, I knew that before."

At last, when the nest was only half finished, the birds lost patience with the conceited empty-head.

"Well, Mistress Mag," cried they, flying away, "as you know all about it, you may e'en finish the nest yourself."

That is the reason the magpie's nest is so badly made.

—FOLK TALE

HOW BUTTERFLIES CAME

One day the flowers flew off their stalks high into the air. They waved their leaves for wings. Because they behaved themselves so well the fairies let them fly again and again, and they no longer had to sit still on their stalks and remain home from morning till night. So by and by their leaves became wings. The flowers had changed into butterflies, red, yellow, and white.

—From Hans Christian Andersen

THE MONKEY DANCES

The organ-grinder called out to the monkey seated on his shoulder, "Dance for the children, Jacko, and I will play."

Jacko swung himself lightly to the sidewalk, pulled off his velvet cap, and bowed low. Then he put the cap on again, pressing it down firmly on his head, and held out his little red skirt with his paws. "Begin," cried his master. And Jacko began to step and turn and slide in time to the music.

The children clapped their hands. Faster and faster went the music and faster and faster went Jacko. At last he spun round and round until he looked like a red top. The music stopped suddenly. Jacko stood motionless on the very tip of his toes. After this he pulled off his cap and bowed low.

"Bravo, Jacko," cried the children, and each threw a penny into his cap for food for himself and his master.

AN APRIL FOOL STORY

One day all the rabbits were close together near a back fence, sitting up on their haunches. The rabbit in the middle was telling the others a story. It was about a rabbit.

"So," said he, going on with the story, "whenever the little rabbit was hungry all he had to say was

'Garden fairy, sweet,

Some lettuce I'd eat,'

And straightway a whole head of lettuce would grow up before him."

"Oh, my," cried all the rabbits together, "how I wish that would happen to me!" And story-teller and all turned a somersault at the very thought of it. After this they sat up again to hear the rest of the story.

But their pink eyes almost burst out of their heads and their ears stood straight up toward the sky. There in front of each was a large leaf of lettuce.

"Why, the story's coming true," cried the story-teller, and he tasted the lettuce. "Yes," said he, "this is real lettuce."

The others were sure of it. They were eating theirs as fast as they could.

Now the dog, who kept the yard, hadn't turned a somersault, so he knew about it. He saw Fred, hiding behind the fence, throw down the lettuce leaves.

"Ha, ha," he barked, "the silly things don't know that to-day is April Fool's Day. Of course," said he, thoughtfully, "they have eaten juicy lettuce leaves. That's not foolish. Fred and I have eaten nothing."

"That story had a happy ending," said the rabbits, as they scampered off to play.

Which do you think was April-fooled?

THE FOOLISH PUPPIES

The biggest puppy said one day to the little puppies, "Let us jump up on the table and enjoy ourselves. There are plenty of bread-crumbs on it. Our mistress has gone out to pay some visits."

The little dogs said, "No, no, no, we will not go. If our mistress should hear of it she would beat us."

"She will know nothing about it," said the other; "come on, the crumbs are fresh and sweet."

"Nay, nay, we must let them alone. We must not go," said the little pups again.

But the big one gave them no peace until at last they went, and got up on the table, and ate up the bread-crumbs with all their might.

While they were at it a shadow of someone passing the window fell on the table. The big pup knew what it meant. He jumped down and made off. But the little pups were caught. Their mistress seized a stick and whipped them out of the room.

Outside the little pups said to the big pup, "Dost, dost, dost, dost thou see?"

But the mean cur gave them no satisfaction. "Didn't, didn't, didn't you expect it?" said he.

So they had to grin and bear it, and make up their minds to be wiser the next time.

A GOLDEN STORY

There was once a buttercup shining in the green grass. "You're a little golden sun that turns everything into gold," said a child who saw it; "perhaps you can tell a golden story."

And would you believe it? The buttercup began without waiting a single moment: "A certain old grandmother sits out of doors every afternoon in her chair. The hands resting in her lap are wrinkled and so is her face, and her hair is as white as the driven snow. All of a sudden two small smooth hands steal round from the back of her chair and cover her eyes. And grandmother immediately says, 'It's my sweet grandchild; I'm sure of it, because she never fails to visit me,' and she reaches up to touch a golden head."

"Why, the story's about me," cried the little girl; "grandmother's guess is never wrong."

But the buttercup went on without pretending to hear. "Then the child runs around in front of the chair and kisses her old grandmother. There is gold in that kiss, I am certain," said the buttercup, "because it leaves a mark of itself on grandmother's face; it smoothes out the wrinkles and it makes her eyes shine with joy.

"That's my golden story," said the buttercup; "every child may go home and play it."

And the little child was happy that what she did had been put into a golden story.

—Hans Christian Andersen

HOW THE CLOCKS PLAYED SCHOOL

Three little clocks sat in a row on the mantelpiece. The servant had put them there to wash their faces, but they made believe they had come to school. The tall grandfather clock from the hall was the teacher. The servant had wheeled him in to sweep behind him, but he too made believe he had come to school.

"Be sure," said Grandfather Clock to his scholars, "that you tell the right time. Everyone in the house looks to you for the time to get up, the time to eat, the time to work, the time to play, and the time to sleep. Is there any little clock here who cannot tell time? All you have to do is to move your hands around your face. When it is time to strike the hour, be sure your large hand is at twelve, and your small hand at the hour. It is very easy."

"Is it, indeed!" said the smallest clock; "how about it when people forget to wind us up?"

"Yes, yes," cried the other two little clocks, "how about that?"

"Silence," cried Grandfather Clock, sternly; "that is a saucy way for little clocks to talk."

At this moment the servant began to wheel Grandfather Clock back into the hall.

"School is out," he said.

So that was the end of it.

HOW MOTHER TABBY PLAYED WITH HER KITTENS

Once three small black kittens begged their mother to play with them. Mother Tabby said nothing, but gave her tail a sly wag to one side. The kittens started back and looked at it. Mother Tabby whisked it over to the other side.

"It is alive," thought the kittens. They arched their backs, and the smallest kitten put out his paw to make it move again. Whack! went Mother Tabby's tail on his nose. The little kitten scampered off.

But he was back again in a minute, and the fun kept up until Mother Tabby walked off as if to say, "It is time for little kittens to be in bed."

THE JOKE

Last Hallowe'en a saucy red apple played a joke. When little Tom ducked for him he bobbed backward and forward so dizzily that little Tom lost his balance and toppled into the tub. The saucy red apple laughed as loudly as any apple can laugh.

But what was that he heard Tom's big brother saying? The big brother had pulled Tom out of the water before you could say "Jack Robinson," and Tom was dripping wet and bawling with fright. What did the saucy red apple hear? It was Tom's big brother saying, "Here, Tom, is a little red apple for you." And he handed the saucy red apple to Tom.

The saucy red apple stopped laughing suddenly, for he found himself between little Tom's sharp teeth.

So Tom had the best of the joke after all, hadn't he?

THE SISTERS

"You dirty black thing," cried the diamond to the coal, "do not come near me."

"I will not indeed," said the coal; "you are too beautiful for the likes of me. I might dim your brilliance."

When she heard this answer, the proud diamond was ashamed of herself. "Press close to me," she said, "you are my own sister. I am only more highly polished."

THE LION AND THE SHEPHERD

Once a lion roaming through the forest trod on a thorn and it stuck in his foot. In great pain he limped out to a shepherd and looked up at him beseechingly. The shepherd gently drew out the thorn. The lion fawned upon him and licked his hand to thank him.

Not long after the shepherd was blamed for a wrong he had not done. The king said he must die. "Throw him to the lions and let him be torn to pieces," commanded the king.

The king's officers seized the poor shepherd and threw him into the arena, before the lion's cage. Out stalked a lion. It was the very one the shepherd had helped. And lo! instead of tearing the shepherd to pieces the noble beast fawned upon him and licked his hand.

The king was amazed. He ordered the shepherd to tell him what it all meant. When he heard he let the shepherd go back to his sheep and the lion back to the free forest.

WHAT HAPPENED TO THE BALLOON

One night a gorgeous balloon when his candle was lighted found himself beside a dull brown acorn.

"What a stupid dolt you are to stay here where you cannot be seen!" he cried, as someone sent him up into the air.

Higher and higher he mounted above the roofs of the houses. "Perhaps he will reach the stars," said the acorn, gazing up after him.

Just then the balloon turned giddy with pride. He reeled, caught fire, and his brief splendor was over.

Years after, in the spot where the acorn had lain that night, a great oak stood up toward heaven and spread his branches wide over the earth.

THE END